DIVORCE
& SPLITTING UP

ADVICE FROM A TOP DIVORCE LAWYER

MARILYN STOWE

Published by Stowe Family Law LLP

DIVORCE
& SPLITTING UP

ADVICE FROM A TOP DIVORCE LAWYER

ISBN 978-0-9576451-0-3

Published by Stowe Family Law LLP.
For more copies of this book, please email chiefexecutive@stowefamilylaw.co.uk.
Tel: 01423 532600

Designed and set by Floyd
www.dearfloyd.com

Printed in Great Britain by CPI Group (UK) Ltd, Croydon, CR0 4YY

Disclaimer
Although every precaution has been taken in the preparation of this book, the publisher
and author assume no responsibility for errors or omissions. Neither is any liability
assumed for damages resulting from the use of this information contained herein.
The contents of this book are intended as general advice and guidance only. Readers
should not place any personal reliance on the material or views expressed, as the law in
this complex area changes frequently. No two cases are ever the same. For specific advice,
you must consult your own solicitor who will be able to give you the best advice based on
the facts of your own case.

This book is dedicated
to my beloved parents,
Arnold and Estelle Morris,

April 2013

Contents

Preface   7

Part I: Let's Stick Together?

2: An Affair: a Death Knell or a Wake-Up Call?   18
3: Can Your Relationship Be Rescued?   29
4: Violence in the Home   38
5: When You Know That It's Over   43
6: Why Separation Doesn't Work   48

Part II: Getting Divorced

7: The Six Steps to Divorce   52
8: What to Do Before You Do Anything Else   61
9: How to Choose a Good Solicitor   80
10: Digging In For Divorce   92
11: Taking Care of Yourself   102

Part III: Cohabitation and Civil Partnerships

12: Cohabitation: What You Need to Know   114
13: Civil Partnerships: What You Need to Know   127

Part IV: International, Expat and Cross-Border Divorce

14: A Note on Divorce in the UK   130
15: Expats and the Dangers of a Place in the Sun   132
16: International Divorce and Children   142

Part V: It's The Money, Honey

17: How It Works   149
18: Order, Order!   177

19: So What Do You Want to Know About Prenuptial
    Agreements?   193
20: Tracking Down Hidden Assets   202
21: How To Keep Your Costs Down   214

Part VI: How To Do Your Best For Your Children

22: You, Your Children and the Law   221
23: Child Support: The Inside Track   238
24: What's the Deal with Dad?   253
25: Helping Your Children Through Divorce   261
26: Grandparents, Stepfamilies and Contact Orders   270

Part VII: What Could Go Wrong?

27: Top Ten Dirty Divorce Tricks   281
28: How to Act in Court: Dos and Don'ts   286
29: Other Pitfalls, and How to Avoid Them   288

Part VIII: How to Move On

30: So I'm Divorced. Now What?   306
31: Setting Yourself Goals for the Future   314

Closing Remarks   316
Useful Resources   319
Acknowledgements   325

Preface

I have spent the last 30 years working only as a divorce lawyer. Before then I regularly handled commercial litigation, some of it international, and I had become accustomed to the tough cut and thrust that came with taking on lawyers worldwide. It wasn't easy; in fact it was extremely stressful, but commercial lawyers aren't paid to have feelings. They are paid to win.

After my son was born in 1988, however, I had to juggle work with my new responsibility as a mother. Something had to give! I could no longer travel as before, I couldn't go to court as much, and I had the responsibility of an office to run - as well as a young baby, a husband and a home to look after. At the same time, perhaps because I had become a parent, I found that I was becoming more involved with family law cases. It is a fascinating area of the law, involving real people with real problems, and I slowly realised that I was well suited to it. I immersed myself in family law. I also read widely around the subject, because I genuinely wanted to help. I wanted my clients to be happy and move on from the despair of marital breakdown.

I also believe that motherhood provided me with revealing insights into the real-life ups and downs of being a parent and managing family relationships when wholly dependent children were involved. I discovered that life was far from easy, and so I decided to advise my clients from my own perspective: *"There but for the grace of... Go us all"*.

It is a fact that life never goes to plan. There are always surprises waiting for us, some happy, some sad. All of us, without exception, will experience the ups and downs of life. But how do we handle them? That is what is important.

The years have since passed by in a flash - and thousands of clients have passed through the doors at Stowe Family Law. I have learned a lot from what I have seen and experienced as a divorce lawyer, and I hope that I can pass at least some of it on to you in this book.

The worst changes to my work that I have experienced have all occurred recently. When I began to practice, all my clients had access to a lawyer. The poorest paid nothing, because legal aid was free. 'Mid-range' clients were still able to secure legal aid, but made contributions. Everybody had access to a lawyer and therefore everybody had access to family law, which was designed to be administered by lawyers and adjudicated by judges.

Times have now changed so much, that hundreds of thousands of people can no longer have access to a lawyer. Instead, they must try and access justice on their own. Family law legal aid has been all but destroyed and I consider this to be a shocking and shameful indictment of our society. At the time of writing, the Government is doing its best to help its citizens help themselves to family law - but its efforts are lame and limp, and its guidance is flimsy.

So I have tried to do something to help. For more than five years now, I have been writing my law blog: www.marilynstowe.co.uk. During that time, I have seen the numbers of visitors rise from 32,000 to 40,000 every month. Every day, I publish posts about new cases, interesting decisions and family law in the news. Subscribers receive free emails, with all the latest posts. Please do take a look if you would like to keep up-to-date with family law developments. I welcome questions from readers and answer as many as I can, free of charge. If you read it together with this book, you will find that my blog explores divorce, splitting up and family law in far more detail than I can do within the confines of these pages.

When I sat down to write this book, I was determined that it would be published at the lowest possible price, so that it could reach the widest audience. I was also determined that it would not be a 'divorce textbook'. Family law is complex. Much can hang upon the wording of a statute or a procedural rule. It isn't always easy to understand – not even for me on occasion, and I have been immersed in family law for decades! Instead I have tried to make this book easy to read and, as much as possible, devoid of legal jargon. I am conscious that many of you, my readers, will be handling your own cases, either because of lack of funds or because you genuinely believe you can make a good fist of it.

This is not one of those interminable tomes written by lawyers, for lawyers. It is my guide to the steps, processes and obstacles that I think you are most likely to meet, along with practical advice for dealing with them. I can't cover every potential challenge that may arise, because everyone's lives are different – and so are their cases. Instead we will look at the most common causes of concern. The process of separating from your spouse or partner can be daunting, and my aim is to make you feel more relaxed and confident, by setting out what you can expect to encounter along the way.

You may not agree with all my advice, and that is your prerogative. I do, however, have a word of warning. Please do try and see a lawyer, if you possibly can. From experience I know that the costs of tailor-made legal advice, from a qualified professional, can be dwarfed by the lifelong financial consequences of doing without it.

After 30 years as a family lawyer, very little shocks me. I have seen clients display outstanding generosity and compassion towards their former partners. I have witnessed vengeful and mean-spirited behaviour. I have seen men and women destroyed by guilt and consumed by betrayal. I have seen others make leaps and bounds towards new, contented lives.

What never ceases to surprise me, however, is the ease with which otherwise successful and confident men and women – and on occasion, their lawyers too! – can make catastrophic errors in the run-up to a split or during divorce proceedings.

Ten Classic Divorce Mistakes

1. **Taking the wrong route.** A 'DIY divorce' is cheap – but expensive in the long run, if you settle for less than you are worth. A collaborative divorce is the perfect answer for some, but an exhausting failure for others. Which path is best for you?
2. **Choosing the wrong solicitor.** Your choice of lawyer will have a significant impact upon your case. Do you know what to look for and what to ask at that all-important first appointment?
3. **Choosing the cheapest solicitor.** This can be a false economy. You may hope to save money by paying rock bottom prices, but if you receive low quality advice in return you can be left with less than your fair share.

It is more important to choose a solicitor in whom you have every confidence.

4. **Thinking that legal aid is available.** It isn't. New legislation, which comes into force in April 2013, is removing certain areas of law from public funding. Family law legal aid is to be limited to cases which involve domestic abuse.

5. **Confusion over prenuptial agreements.** This takes two forms: believing that a prenuptial agreement is valid when it isn't, or believing that a prenuptial agreement cannot be upheld when it can be. In a landmark case called Radmacher v Granatino, heard by the Supreme Court in 2010, a prenuptial agreement was upheld. Since then the courts have been more willing to give "decisive weight" to prenups, but that doesn't mean prenups are always worth the paper on which they are written.

6. **Hiding money.** What happens when you are caught? The answer: any existing court order can be overturned, and you can be landed with a hefty bill. Some of the busiest team members at our firm are the forensic accountants, who specialise in tracking down secret bank accounts and other assets.

7. **Adopting other underhand tactics.** Many of these are illegal, will reflect badly upon the culprit in court and may land him or her with criminal charges. Other actions are grey areas. Do you know what is allowed and what is not?

8. **Settling your finances before you are ready.** Timing is essential. Settle too early before all the assets

have been fully investigated, and you may settle for too little. Settle too late and circumstances may have altered irrevocably. An economic recession or upturn can have major effects upon a case. And don't settle because of financial pressure. Your lawyer really can advise you through it all.

9. **Thinking you know it all.** The truth is that unless you are a divorce lawyer, you don't. You wouldn't pull your own teeth out, would you? Or conduct an appendectomy on yourself? So why do you think you can provide your own legal counsel?

10. **Being an ostrich.** I know it is tough, but if your partner insists the relationship has broken down, don't bury your head in the sand and refuse to accept the decision. You may only make the process – and your bank statements – more painful in the long run.

One of my reasons for writing this book is to prevent others from leaping into a decision to divorce that they may come to regret, or making blunders such as those outlined above. With knowledge and guidance, such events and developments can be avoided.

Another reason is that family law is changing, fast. Over the past few years there have been momentous changes to the laws governing a couple's finances, property and any children they have. Campaigns for fathers' rights continue to gather steam and are already producing positive results.

All this, at a time when relationships and families are themselves facing significant changes and challenges. New social mores have transformed expectations. New technol-

ogies have transformed the ways in which people meet and communicate with one another.

It is a sad fact that more than half of marriages will end in divorce. There are 120,000 divorces every year in England and Wales; for cohabiting couples, the rate of relationship breakdown is even higher. Hundreds of thousands of children are affected. As a result of the turbulent economic climate, the rate of relationship breakdown is predicted to soar in coming years.

Modern relationships have become shifting tides, but some truths remain constant. In love, happy endings are not guaranteed.

For most people, separation and divorce are deeply unpleasant experiences. Nobody enjoys a divorce. I have yet to meet anyone who has been through the process and describes it as easy. Furthermore, no divorcing couple will ever view the split from the same perspective. The objective is to stand back and to try and consider both points of view. Once you can do that, you are closer to resolution.

If you are getting a divorce or heading towards one, I hope that this book can be your map. Case studies, checklists, worksheets, insider's tips and pointers will help you to face the realities. If you decide to proceed, this book will guide you through those choppy waters, and out the other side. You don't have to agree with all my advice and besides, not all of it will be applicable to your case, but at the very least I hope that I can point you in the right direction.

I have often observed that clients who are knowledgeable and well-prepared, with a realistic outlook, are better equipped to cope with proceedings and move on with their lives afterwards.

Yesterday cannot be changed. Tomorrow can be.
Marilyn Stowe, December 2012

Part I: Let's Stick Together?

1: Making a Difficult Decision

CASEBOOK

Mrs L was an attractive woman in her mid-forties. Sitting in my office with her head bowed, twisting a damp tissue in her lap, she told me about her husband. He had recently departed the marital home and moved in with another woman – but Mrs L refused to accept that her marriage was over. Hopeful that he would return, she told me that in her opinion, the marriage could be salvaged.

It didn't help that that the errant husband telephoned her frequently, hinting that one day he might come back. I have encountered a number of these manipulative spouses: they pull all the strings, but like to distance themselves from any blame. So they behave badly and blow hot and cold, pushing their exasperated partners to issue divorce proceedings. In this case, Mrs L had made an appointment with me at a friend's behest. However it appeared that she considered divorce to be a tentative and 'second best' option.

When it came to her broken marriage, Mrs L was in denial. This is common among both men and women: the initial shock of revelation can give way to depres sion. When emotions run high, it can be difficult to think rationally. This means that in spite of all the evidence, it may be difficult to see the wood for the trees.

I felt that Mrs L needed some help and I referred her to a local therapist. However I feared that if too much time passed and no action was taken, her husband could use the situation to his advantage. He would have time to buy another home, establish a higher set of outgoings and pay away money that he would otherwise have to pass to his wife. He could also rearrange his finances. If he did -and often the trick used is to turn liquid assets illiquid - it could prove to be a great problem.

Mrs L was happy to make an appointment with the therapist. As for the divorce: she said she would consider it. As she left my office, I had the distinct impression that she would do no such thing. She wanted her husband to return. But if he showed no signs of doing so, and her pleas fell on deaf ears, she would somehow have to accept that the decision to end her marriage had already been taken and that she had played no part in it.

Nobody who gets married plans to divorce. When couples pledge *"until death do us part"*, they tend to mean it. But life brings unexpected temptations and unforeseen pressures. People change. Relationships wither.

A marriage that appears to be completely happy on the surface may be disrupted and destroyed by the intervention of a third party, even though such an event was neither sought nor anticipated by either spouse.

Even so, it is rare for marriages to collapse without warning. Instead they tend to crumble over a protracted period. Couples lose interest in each other. They take one another for granted. They stop trying. We've all seen such couples on the high street. One partner is immaculately groomed and looking smart; the other is slobbing alongside, in a scruffy tracksuit and trainers. There can grow feelings of resentment, isolation, anger and frustration. Boredom is likely to set in. Perhaps there is frustration at work as well. Perhaps a temptation will arise and will prove too difficult to resist.

I long ago concluded that divorce arises and is propelled by uncontrollable human instincts including self-preservation, protection and survival. A person going through divorce, whether they admit it or not, is forced to think almost exclusively of what is in his or her best interests. People are not perfect. Human instinct in a survival situation isn't about continuing to hunt with the rest of the pack, meekly obeying society's customs. It is about making private decisions to tackle lonely challenges .

Will you stay or will you go? Are you wavering, or have you made a firm decision? How can you know that your choice is the 'right' one?

Splitting up shouldn't be the first resort. Every avenue should be explored before a decision is made to bring the marriage to an end.

2: An Affair: a Death Knell or a Wake-Up Call?

CASEBOOK

Mr B came to see me because his wife was seeing another man. The couple, both in their early 50s, led busy lives and their three children had all left home. The wife had a full-time job and over the previous six months, she had become increasingly remote. Her behaviour had deteriorated and she had become argumentative, irrational and rude. He dreaded her presence, as she kept picking arguments and finding fault with him. He told me he felt utterly lost.

When Mr B tackled his wife with his suspicions of an affair, she more or less confirmed them. In that he was fortunate; most people, when confronted about an illicit liaison, will deny it.

My client saw no hope for his marriage. His trust and faith in his wife had shattered. He had no wish to 'rebuild' his broken life with her. The wife, too, had signalled the end of the partnership. She had no desire to sleep with her husband, or to share her life with him. She had emotionally and physically committed herself elsewhere. She was being faithful and monogamous, but to another person. An affair had ended this marriage for good.

Some relationships can survive affairs but as a divorce lawyer, I tend to see the destructive effects of extra-marital liaisons. I see clients who have not been able to cope after learning of a partner's adultery. They have endured their suspicions, but knowing of the affair has effectively terminated the marriage. In all these cases, the damage has been done. It has destroyed the trust that glued the relationship together. At least one party considers the marriage over and wants out.

At other times: well, it is not hard to tell if a client is having an affair, and it is not hard to tell if somebody is holding back the truth. I don't make moral judgements about a client's behaviour; instead, my role is to do the best that I can for them.

Lipstick on your cyber collar

Have you noticed that modern technology has changed the ways in which affairs are conducted? Mobile phones, e-mail and social media sites all lend themselves to private communications, away from prying eyes and ears. Dating sites and forums are gateways to new liaisons. However, modern technology's 'footprint' – its trail of evidence – is not difficult to follow.

One or two of my well-known sportsmen clients found themselves in the divorce courts after they sent flirty text messages arranging illicit liaisons to their wives, instead of the intended recipients. Brawn doesn't always equal brains!

One report has claimed that nearly a quarter of all married couples admit to snooping on one another's emails and text messages. If you are getting divorced, however, please note that there can be legal implications to such behaviour.

CASEBOOK

Ms J was a smart, successful lawyer. Our meeting began very calmly and her problem soon became clear.

She was married to a chartered accountant. They had three children, aged between eight and 14. The family enjoyed an affluent lifestyle and had no particular worries. On the surface, all was well. She certainly hadn't been looking for romance outside her marriage. Unfortunately, it arrived in the guise of an old university friend. He was the MD of a successful business. He had a family, but had long since divorced his own wife. They 'clicked' and embarked on a passionate affair. Ms J's husband noticed that she had become withdrawn and was worried about her, but suspected nothing.

Ms J wanted advice on the likely outcome of a divorce. When I asked how she thought divorce would affect her family, she burst into tears and her control slipped. All her guilt came tumbling out. She said quite simply that it would devastate them all.

I answered her questions and explained that from a practical perspective, a divorce would not be a problem. Financially, the family would be fine. I advised her about the divorce process, the process for a financial settlement, the law about children, the likely costs and how it all worked in practice.

Then I gave Ms J the advice I suspected she really sought. I told her not to do it.

I drew upon my experience gained from years spent

listening to clients' problems and told her that I thought she still had the chance to salvage her marriage. I advised her to ditch the other man and, if necessary, change her job or even initiate a career move. Although the pain of saying goodbye to the other man would be very, very tough, it would be nothing like the pain she could bring upon her family if the affair continued. She said she had "ripped the lid from Pandora's box". I told her she could - and should - put it back on again.

Time will tell which part of my advice she has taken.

Dear Marilyn

My husband is having an affair - I'm pretty sure of it. The signs are all there, including unexplained entries on credit card statements, for clothes boutiques and flowers. He has been out wining and dining but not with me; I have heard him whispering into his mobile phone and seen him texting when he thought I was downstairs. I feel that I must seriously consider divorce, because he is behaving badly to me as well.

Should I consult a divorce lawyer now, before my husband suspects that I'm onto him? Would this give me an advantage, in case I do decide to go ahead with proceedings? Or should I first confront him with my suspicions, to give him the chance to explain and make amends?

What would you do, if you were me?

Daphne

Dear Daphne

First things first: from a legal perspective, your husband's behaviour is unreasonable and is sufficient to get divorced. But that is too drastic a step right now, unless he is trying to manoeuvre you into divorce. Is he?

I believe you should talk to him. You should talk as calmly as possible and discuss how you see your marriage. This will give him an opening to talk to you, if that is what he seeks, but you should be prepared for him to open up about his unhappiness. At least you will know the truth, and that must be better than carrying on in limbo.

You should also be prepared for the reaction, "You are paranoid! There's nothing wrong." As the wife you may be the last to know, especially if he isn't yet certain of what he wants.

I believe that it is always better to be informed than it is to dwell in ignorance and misplaced hope. That you have been moved to write to me suggests that you are already considering your situation very carefully. See your lawyer.

Marilyn

Early Warning Signs

After 20 years as a divorce lawyer I have heard all the excuses and all the explanations. Given that we are all different as individuals, it is surprising how many of us tend to follow the same, habitual patterns of behaviour. So, how do you know if your partner is planning to leave you? In my experience, these are some of the common early warning signs.

Checklist:
Ten ways to tell if he is cheating on you

1. **He starts taking an unusual interest in his clothes and overall appearance.** You have nagged him for years about boring suits and stained ties. You have urged him to adopt a trendier hairstyle and told him that unwanted facial hair really isn't a turn-on. Now he's taking action on his own - and alarm bells are ringing.

2. **He becomes very protective of his mobile phone.** How many times has a client told me about a spouse who behaves oddly and maintains a death grip on their mobile phone? The answer is far too many to remember! So far as marital breakdown is concerned, such activities have become epidemic. One client of mine became suspicious after her husband began sleeping with his mobile under his pillow. One night, when she could stand it no longer, she manoeuvred it from beneath his sleeping head, crept downstairs, read the text messages from his lover - and woke him with her noisy demands for a divorce.

3. **He takes out new credit cards in his name only and you never see the monthly bills.** This is a sure sign that he is spending money on things he doesn't want you to know about. He's probably going to try and

put some of the expenses through his business, so he'll be keeping the receipts somewhere.

4. **He suddenly starts spending nights away from home *"on business"*.** He claims that his new position at work means he has to travel more frequently. Don't call him at the hotel as he will be with clients all night. He will call you when he's free. Really he will!

5. **He takes an unusual amount of interest in your dietary regime and signs up at the local gym.** After years during which his only exercise was carrying his beer to an armchair in front of the football, he is now desperate to regain his youth.

6. **He begins to make snide and hurtful remarks about you and your views when in company.** Feeling guilty about his affair, the only way he can justify his behaviour is to pretend to himself that you forced him into it by treating him badly. If his comments goad you into responding in kind, he can convince himself that it is all your fault.

7. **He begins to drop the name of a female colleague into everyday conversation.** Subconsciously he's comparing her with you. And it gives him a feeling of power: *"I'm so clever/powerful that I can drop the name of my mistress into conversation and not get found out"*.

8. **He begins intercepting the postman and says he'll check the bank statements during a spare half hour at work.** He's read all about men who get caught out by their wives finding hotel receipts in suit pockets, so he's paying for everything in cash. If he

keeps the bank statements you won't find out how frequently he visits the cash point.

9. **He trades in the family saloon for something sportier.** The trusty Ford/Vauxhall has always suited you in the past, but now the children have grown up, he says it's time to begin enjoying yourselves. James at work says the Porsche Boxster is such fun and so economical to run. Just try asking to borrow it for an evening...

10. **He suggests separate holidays.** He is so busy at work that he cannot take time off. But you and the kids should go; you can even take your parents and he'll pay. While you're away he won't have to rush those illicit meetings with his lover.

11. **Sex is a definite no.** Even he won't try the headache routine; it's not the kind of thing a 'macho stud' like him would say. However, he becomes incredibly understanding and sympathetic when he can tell that you are tired, have had a bad day or have an early start in the morning. Anything to avoid physical contact.

Here, in the interests of sexual equality, are ten ways for a man to tell if a woman is having an affair.

Checklist:
Ten ways he can tell you're cheating on him

1. **The mobile phone bill goes missing.** If lengthy calls to your lover have sent the telephone bill spiralling upwards, the last thing you want is for your husband to

discover that nearly all the calls have been made to just one number. Worse than that, you definitely don't want him calling that number! So you get a pay-as-you-go mobile. Why?

2. **You stop cooking for him.** If he gets home, asks what you've made for dinner and you reply, *"I've made reservations"*, he knows he's in trouble.

3. **You often talk about how good the window cleaner is,** how the tennis coach has really improved your game or why the builders need to stay longer than intended. The wife of a rich, successful man, if she feels neglected and second-best to the attractions of work, may find solace with a lover who has far less material wealth but does not substitute financial rewards for affection and attention.

4. **You really don't care how his day went at work!** The conversation and gossip about his work once fascinated you. Now it bores you to tears. You are no longer interested in his work because you are no longer interested in him. It shows.

5. **You look younger and trimmer - and he still hasn't noticed!** If he no longer notices your hair, make-up or figure, he will probably be slow to twig that someone else has. By the time reality has dawned, it may be too late.

6. **You are suddenly spending more time with girl-friends.** You suggest a separate bank account for your 'girly' indulgences, so that you don't have to bother him all the time. At least that's what you want him to believe. But what will happen if he finds your bank state-

ments or discovers your PIN number?

7. **When work commitments prevent him from coming on holiday, you are unusually understanding.** You tell him that you'll enjoy the sun and finally read all those unopened books. Instead, you plan to meet up with the guy he had dismissed as a beach bum on your last trip together to the Caribbean. You tell him that you know he is too busy to call - and that you'll ring him.

8. **You begin to wear younger, sexier clothing.** He is long past noticing anything new you wear, although when he does he is quick to complain about the cost. You are careful if you use the joint account to pay for them. You always tell him what you have bought, even if you don't tell him why.

9. **You are embarrassed in his company.** Suddenly he can't do anything right in your eyes. His fashion sense belongs to a different age, his jokes aren't funny anymore and you begin to compare him - unfavourably - with more dynamic and successful friends and colleagues.

10. **Sex is a definite no.** The headache excuse is so see-through, it's transparent. You've tried the one about being worried that the children will hear. Perhaps the gym or the tennis has tired you. Perhaps there is a late-night television programme you really can't miss.

When there are more than two people in your marriage, there will come a time when these excuses run out. Then you will have to decide whether to stay or to go.

Be warned: it is a bad mistake to leave a boring spouse who

loves you, if good sex is all that you have in common with a new partner. In my experience far too many people have made that mistake, divorced and ended up alone and embittered.

3: Can Your Relationship Be Rescued?

Perhaps a subtitle for this chapter should be: And in your heart of hearts, do you want to rescue it?

If the answer is *"yes"*, the first step is to recognise – as soon as possible - when the marriage begins to go wrong. Because you are reading this book, I'm going to presume that you have already taken this first step.

The second step is to decide, as a couple, to do something about it. If only one of you wants to save the relationship, it isn't going to happen.

A relationship can only be rescued and revived when both parties believe that it is worth fighting for. Even then, it can only be saved when both parties are committed to that fight. There is a world of difference between a genuine desire to work to save a marriage when it is the shared aim of both parties, and when it is a hope and a prayer existing in one mind only.

I am not a therapist, but I do spend my days working with couples in conflict. I have learned that more often than not, the ultimate reason for the breakdown of a relationship is a symptom of that breakdown, rather than a cause. So an adulterous affair that brings about a divorce may not be the initial cause of that divorce: the marriage may, to all intents and purposes, have broken down beforehand.

I advocate holding a marriage together whenever possible, assuming the co-operation and willingness of both parties. The grass elsewhere is not always as green as it may seem. A subsequent marriage is just as likely - more likely, in fact - to founder.

At some stage, you and your partner must have been happy together. You must have been in love and you must have been sexually attracted to each other. Perhaps you enjoyed your relationship sufficiently to have children together. Can those feelings be recaptured?

CASEBOOK

Mrs Y came to see me after her 55-year-old husband left her for his 23-year-old girlfriend. Mrs Y told me that he was anxious about getting old, and was used to getting his own way, He was besotted with his new girlfriend, and was delighted that she wished to have children with him. He had made the decision to give up his wife, his two sons and all they shared as a family. He told Mrs Y that if he didn't grasp this fabulous opportunity to sail off into the sunset with his young lady love, life wouldn't be worth living.

When I listen to some of my female clients talk about their partners, I can't help but wonder: is there such a thing as a 'Man-o-Pause'? This particular affliction, if it exists, affects high-powered men of a certain age. If you are an alpha male, used to being revered and treated as His Majesty the King at home and at work, you deal with boredom by creating challenges. You take deliberate risks. You love the thrill of the chase. You want it all. You want to eat your cake and have it. You certainly don't want a longstanding, dutiful, apparently dull wife getting in the way. Or so you think.

If I could, I would diagnose my very own treatment for this condition. I would tell the sufferer: this is the 21st century. You are not King Henry VIII. You are a married man with a family and a job at which you are successful. You have an enviable lifestyle. You should do what it takes to preserve what you have. Make a tough call. Turn your back on your femme fatale and say goodbye to the thrills of sex with her (which, over time, would have palled anyway). The heady excitement of that illicit affair will recede and become a memory. Rekindle your sex life with your wife. You aren't her brother and she isn't your sister, even if it seems that way. Appreciate the role she plays in your life and how she helps to hold your home and your family together.

If that didn't work, I would advise him that his man-o-pause would cost him dearly. I would warn him that he risked an expensive second divorce once he became too old in body and mind for his new lady love. I would describe the significant divorce payouts he could expect to make to both his former wives and for their respective children. Much of what he had earned would cease to be his.

However I was advising Mrs Y – not her husband. The advice I gave her must have sounded unusual, coming from a divorce lawyer, because it didn't sound to me likeshe wanted a divorce at all. I told her to go home and fight for her man as best she could. A man-o-pause, like a female menopause, fades with time.

The biggest challenge is not recognising problems within a relationship, but knowing what to do about them. Often it is too trite simply to say *"try harder"* or *"keep your sense of humour"* or *"respect one another"*. At the end of this book I have listed some 'Useful Resources', including marriage counselling services, which can equip you with all you need to give your relationship another go. If you try your best but are unable to make your marriage work by yourselves, what do you have to lose if you ask for extra help with your efforts?

Dear Marilyn

What's the secret of a happy relationship? I would really like to know, because my own marriage is filled with ups and downs. It isn't good for us, and it isn't fair on our children. I have considered divorce a number of times and have even consulted a divorce lawyer before now, although I have never been able to go through with it. But I'm not sure we can go on like this.

Penny

Dear Penny,

I am married myself and like most of us, I am a romantic at heart. I think the best relationships, the ones that last for life, are created when both partners want and do more for one another than they want and do for themselves, A shared sense of humour also plays an important role. Even when I am in the crossest of moods, my husband can always make me laugh. If you still have that spark, you can make it.

This doesn't mean that your relationship will be perfect. But continuing to give and to put one another first will help to keep your relationship in good health. It isn't always easy. Most of us are quite selfish but, if we consciously force ourselves to put the other person first, there is a really good chance of success. If a couple stops doing these things for one another - or even if just one of them stops - the relationship will falter and grind to a halt.

When I apply this test to people I know, some of them married for many years and others who are clients, either getting divorced or thinking about it, it rings true every time.

Marilyn

Modern lives

There have been momentous changes to the concept of 'the family' over the years, and profound changes to the established family structure within marriage. Divorce no longer carries the social stigma that it once did. Even so, many people live together with no intention of entering into marriage. They don't see the need. Many of those who do marry have no religious or social conviction that requires them to marry for life, for better or for worse.

There can be little doubt that social changes and liberalised attitudes have been as beneficial as they have been welcome. My only qualm is that as a divorce lawyer, I often encounter the presumption that if and when a relationship ends, the partners can move on without fuss. This is a dangerous presumption because in real life, few relationships end in such a casual way.

No man – or woman – is an island. No relationship exists in a vacuum. Today's relationships may be more diverse and more complex than those of previous generations, but when they break down they do so with many of the same problems.

The irony is that even in these liberal times, it is still the law that creates the canvas upon which all our lives are drawn. Sometimes it can seem that the law is several steps behind society when recognising and dealing with the pace of change.

If you cannot make up your mind about your relationship, and splitting up or getting divorced is beginning to sound like the 'easy' option, think again and think carefully. I do not say this because I believe that you could or should remain with your current partner or spouse. I say this because if you do decide that separate paths will suit you best, you should know that those paths may be rocky.

When you make your decision, look to the future as well as the present. What do you see there?

Christmas is a time for living

I don't believe in 'Divorce D-Day': the first Monday back to work in January, when family lawyers are supposed to have their busiest day of the year. They claim to be inundated with new instructions following the Christmas holidays but as far as I am concerned, 'Divorce D-Day' is simply PR hype to drum up work for lawyers.

At the same time, I am in no doubt that the festive season

heightens stress levels in households up and down the country. One year I saw four new women clients in the two weeks before Christmas. One had grown-up children and wanted to initiate divorce proceedings before Christmas. The other three all had young families; they were determined to proceed, but decided to wait until a few weeks so that they did not spoil their children's holidays.

Without exception, all four ladies were dreading the annual festivities; the client with grown-up children told me that she wished to avoid them completely. They described the hard slog: all the preparation beforehand, the shopping, the cooking and the day itself. One mentioned the sausage rolls; another, the puddings begun in early November. All complained about the hard work, cooking all the food and serving it in nice clothes that were bound to get gravy-stained. They described the tidying that had to be fitted around entertaining, the exhaustion and the never-ending rounds of relations and friends for at least a week afterwards. Even in this day and age, with the drive for equality, more than one of the women told me that she had to do all the work herself - and dreaded it. None of them would put themselves through it at all if their children were older.

Listening to these tales of drudgery, it seems to me that for many women who take on the chores year in, year out, Christmas continues to be an exhausting, miserable slog. I can't help concluding that it isn't the festive season that causes a divorce. It's the thought of it.

If the prospect of Christmas is making you or your spouse anxious, and it is possible to do something practical to relieve pressure and save someone's sanity at this time of the year

- please, do it! Can you enlist help from their loved ones? If money isn't an issue, can you pay others to come and help make Christmas as painless as possible? Or why not go away over the Christmas period, and let others take on the burden?

I can't guarantee that it will make everything perfect, but the cost is far, far cheaper than a divorce.

Marilyn's marriage mantras

Tell yourself: the grass is not always greener on the other side. All my years of working in divorce suggest that within a few years the same patterns repeat themselves.

Tell yourself: there is a difference between doing right and wrong.

Tell yourself: you are going to hold your head high and set your family a standard.

Tell yourself: throwing away an investment of 10, 15, 20 years or more is madness.

Tell yourself: you can't have everything you want.

Tell yourself: life is about how you react to a challenge.

Tell yourself: if you are bored or depressed, is a divorce really the answer? Or could another change of lifestyle have the same intended effect?

Tell yourself: accept what you have, and cherish it.

Tell yourself: value the good that is in your life already.

Talk to one another! Discuss your feelings. Take your time; don't rush. Explain why you are so morose, sullen and uncommunicative. Discuss how saving your marriage can preserve the set up you thought would be there forever.

Don't expect miracles, but don't let anger take over. Don't lay blame. It's a waste of time. Remember what brought you together in the first place. Look for the good in one another, rather than the bad. Can you still laugh together? Have you really reached the end of the road? Or has the road turned a sharp corner? Don't look back. Look forward.

Not everyone is emotionally strong enough to take the pain for continuing gain. Not everyone believes that the ups and downs of years spent with an equal partner are worth preserving. Not everyone knows that sometimes - just some-times - what we have only becomes really valuable when we are about to lose it.

And if it is just too late for this, and you know or feel that your relationship cannot, should not or will not go on? If that is the case, please keep reading.

4: Violence in the Home

Some readers will be bemused by the inclusion of a chapter on domestic abuse within this section of the book, which is about making your mind up about the future of your marriage. In such cases it's a no-brainer, surely? For many of those who experience violence, however, the decision to break free remains a difficult one.

Divorce lawyers hear stories of extreme violence practically every day of the week, told to them by women (and men) seeking help in the form of non-molestation orders and occupation orders on family homes. It is relatively common to meet bruised and battered women with bitten faces or broken jaws, who seek urgent help. At its worst, violence within the home ends with women paying the ultimate price: two women every week are killed by a current or former partner.

If you are a victim of domestic violence, please know that family lawyers are not permitted to breach professional privilege. This means that what you tell your lawyer remains within those four walls. Confidentiality is assured.

CASEBOOK

Mrs A's husband broke her nose and jaw. She began divorce proceedings because she felt that she could not carry on. The couple had been married for ten years and had two children, aged eight and five.

She told me that her husband was "perfectly nor-

---

mal" most of the time but that on occasion, "something would come over him". He would become angry and let rip. During the marriage Mrs A had sustained a black eye, a broken finger, a torn lip and bruises on her body. The children had witnessed the violence. On a couple of occasions she'd had to spend time in bed to recover. This time, however, she felt that he had gone too far. She came to see me after discharging herself from hospital.

After obtaining a non-molestation order, Mrs A began divorce proceedings. Her husband vowed never to beat her again. He sent her flowers and cried in front of her, telling her that he would kill himself if she did not return. Two weeks later and with many apologies, Mrs A decided to withdraw proceedings "for the sake of the children".

She was in the throes of recovery from physical pain and substantial emotional blackmail, but she decided to withdraw after considering her options long and hard. As I noted previously, I don't pass judgement on any of my clients – but I couldn't help concluding that Mrs A was simply too weak and too worn down to continue.

That was ten years ago. Since then this pattern has been repeated every six months or so, and her file is now thick. Mrs A will contact us, but she will then pull out and refuse to let us proceed. It is extremely frustrating and depressing for us because we could do so much to improve her situation, but she will not leave her husband. Perhaps he will die before she does, and she will *get her release that way.*

Worse still, I hope she doesn't snap. Sometimes the abused person in a relationship - man or woman - just cannot take it anymore. The abuser is found dead; the abused is charged with manslaughter or murder.

Remember: a leopard never changes its spots. If you are the victim of violence, no matter how hard it is and no matter how many excuses you make, my advice is straightforward. Get out. It is nonsense to say that you are staying put for the sake of the children. You should remove them from this abusive relationship as quickly as you can.

Find the strength to do it; if you can't, find someone professional to help you.

The legal remedies

If you seek a divorce, you usually do so after considering every possible alternative and reaching a reasoned, but painful conclusion that life cannot go on as it is. Emergency orders, on the other hand, are by their very nature obtained at a time of great need. If you seek an emergency order, you do so out of panic and fear.

- The legal process is designed to assist quickly. Family lawyers are trained to work speedily and outside of normal office hours.
- The court system is geared to process emergency order applications as swiftly as possible: the process can be completed within a day.

- A non-molestation order prohibits the abuser from molesting you or, in certain circumstances, your children. The abuser may not damage or dispose of your possessions. The abuser may not instruct anyone else to harass, intimidate or use violence against you. Such an order is relatively easy to obtain.

- An occupation order may prevent your abuser from remaining in your home or coming near it. It may order the abuser to stay in restricted parts of the house, or to let you enter the property if he or she has locked you out. Such an order may be sought if the relationship is characterised by extreme violence, or if the abuser's presence causes immense distress to you or your children. Please note that even if an occupation order is in place, the court can order the abuser to continue paying for the property's monthly outgoings.

- A person who breaches an order has committed a criminal offence and can be jailed for contempt. In certain cases the police can be ordered to arrest them immediately and bring them before the court.

- If you are abused and battered, the law is there to help you and to keep you as safe as possible. The police should be contacted immediately; at the very least they will ensure that there is no breach of the peace. In serious cases they will begin criminal proceedings against the aggressor.

- One major criticism of the system is that those who experience violence may receive little or no obvious backup from the police, if an order is not in place. The stock phrase? *"Go and get an order, love; there is nothing we can do without it"*. A desperate woman will not know whether this is true or false. In fact it is false.

• Legal remedies do work, but only when you are fiercely committed to them and you are determined to see everything through. Capitulation and a 'fresh start' may seem like the easy way out – but only until the next time. My advice to those who are suffering is to think positively and to do something about it now. The next time may be the last time.

5: When You Know That It's Over

Checklist:
You know you're done when:

- You want out of your marriage or relationship because the thought of spending the rest of your life with your current partner makes you shudder. You may or may not have someone else in the wings.
- Your partner has betrayed you and you cannot forgive them. The trust between you both has broken down to such an extent that, even with counselling, you cannot fathom how that trust can ever be rebuilt.
- Your partner's behaviour has left you with little choice.
- Your partner has requested a 'trial separation'. (See the next chapter.)
- You have sat back and taken a long look at the pros and cons of each of your options, perhaps with the help of a close friend, a GP or a counsellor. As a result, you picture yourself happier out of the marriage than in it.
- You discuss the situation with your partner and reach a mutual decision: it's over.
- You were planning to stay together for the children, but the relationship has deteriorated to such an extent that your children ask you to consider splitting up.
- There is nothing left between you.
- Your partner wants out of the relationship. This is often the most difficult reason to accept. Do you truly love your partner? If you did, wouldn't you let go?

CASEBOOK

Mr W believed that his wife was going through the menopause and/or having a nervous break-down. She nagged him, complained that he spent too much time in the pub and had moved into their guest bedroom, ostensibly because of his snoring. Mr W came to see me at the suggestion of his friends.

As the catalogue of his wife's criticisms and slights unfurled, I began to suspect that she was having an affair. It isn't normal to move out of the bedroom. And why had his friends recommended a visit to a divorce lawyer? Friends often detect what is going on, and often know more than they say.

Mr W was certain that his wife's behaviour was all his fault. He wanted to know, what could he do better? I was frank with him. I told that, although I could well be mistaken, it sounded to me as if his wife was comparing him to another man.

He returned a few months later, to let me know that my hunch had been right. He wanted to begin divorce proceedings.

Despite my frankness with this client, I do feel that such cases have to be handled carefully. When people feel that they have been made fools of, it up-sets them terribly and can make them angry and vengeful. When you know that it's over, honesty is the best policy.

The hurt of false hope

In human and emotional terms, divorce cases can be divided up into three categories: amicable, acrimonious and agonising.

The first, in which both parties agree that their relationship has run its full course, is probably the easiest. The second, in which one partner has treated the other so badly that reconciliation is simply not worthy of consideration, can be the nastiest but is still relatively clean cut.

The third is the saddest of all. One partner wants a divorce and the other doesn't. The refusenik partner denies that the marriage is over, and puts up every possible obstacle to the divorce taking place. This is done out of sheer bloody-mindedness, or because the partner still harbours the vain hope of a future reconciliation, even to the point of ignoring the pile of solicitors' letters that has built up beneath the letterbox.

This approach, while understandable from an emotional point of view, can be very expensive in terms of both health and finance. Years of constant stress and turmoil, caused by this denial of reality, can take its toll on even the fittest and most well-balanced of people. A nervous breakdown can be the end result.

Sadly, if your partner is set on dissolving the relationship, there is little point to your efforts to keep that relationship going indefinitely. It doesn't often happen that both people agree the marriage has broken down and go their separate ways. Often that decision is made by one person only. The other has no choice but to accept that decision, with the greatest sadness.

Dear Marilyn

My partner of 20 years has informed me that she does not wish our relationship to continue. To say I am stunned is an understatement. I always thought we were very happy together, so this decision of hers has come completely out of the blue. She says that she has made up her mind, but I am less than convinced. Surely, with all that we have shared, we must have something worth holding onto? How can I make her see this?

John

Dear John,

I knew one man who was utterly shocked when his wife left him after 30 years of marriage. This man had a difficult personality. His wife waited until the kids grew up, and then she was off. I'll bet that although he didn't see it coming, those around him did. You must take off the blinkers. I also recommend that you and your partner seek counselling as a matter of urgency. Counselling can encourage some people to review their decisions; for others, it merely confirms their determination to move on. If your partner remains keen to end the relationship, it is her decision and it is one that you must come to terms with.

Marilyn

If it comes to it and divorce is the only available option, how do you deal with this unwelcome reality? There is, I think, only one way. Take it right on the chin. Life is made up of happy events and unhappy events. Your responses and your ability to cope determine your personality and your character. If I was a philosopher instead of a lawyer, I would propose that life is a series of tests. It is how you deal with each test that determines the kind of individual you are. Taking it on the chin, however, still requires you to grieve for your relationship. You need to grieve, to be able to move forward. It will take time and you will go through a range of deep feelings. Tell yourself to expect this, that it is normal. And if you feel you need to, take expert advice. Help yourself to accept what has happened.

6: Why Separation Doesn't Work

I do not like the concept of 'separation': when a couple agrees to live apart from one another for a temporary or extended period. I see it as a halfway house offering little if any consolation to either party, for the following reasons:

1. **It is not necessary for divorce.** The idea that you have to separate before you can get a divorce is a myth that is seemingly perpetuated by every pub lawyer in the land. It is true that two years of separation, providing both parties consent, can be one of the 'facts' used to prove that 'irretrievable breakdown' of the marriage has taken place. It is also true that if there is no consent, then the couple must live apart for five years before one of them can seek a divorce against the other's will. However, as detailed in chapter 7, - these are not the only 'facts'.

2. **In my opinion, it is impossible to recover from the effect of a broken relationship** during a period of separation. Both parties are leading completely separate lives, meeting different people and perhaps becoming romantically involved with others. At the same time they are not truly free, whether they consented to the separation or not, because they are not yet divorced. In surveys of situations that cause the most stress to people, divorce regularly comes second only to the death of a spouse. In a way, divorce can be compared with bereavement: the body has to be buried before one can even begin to think about getting over a death. Divorce

is a way of breaking with the past.

3. **Sometimes one partner has decided that the marriage or relationship has come to an end,** but cannot bring themselves to tell their partner the awful truth. Instead, this person hides behind the charade of a separation.

"Let's see how it works out for the next few months", they say, giving false hopes and dreams to their partner. Months later, when these dreams are shattered, it is at a substantial emotional cost to the partner who worried, waited and hoped because they were not in a position to accept the blindingly obvious.

I believe that if a marriage is going to succeed it does so with both parties living together. If neither party can live with the other, or if one party feels that the marriage is over, then the kindest way out is to end that marriage as quickly as possible. Sometimes it is necessary to be cruel to be kind.

A Deed of Separation

If you do wish to separate from your spouse, however, it is a relatively simple process. You can enter into a physical separation, which you can do while still living in the same house. In addition to this, or instead of it, you can enter into a Deed of Separation.

A Deed of Separation records your agreement to separate, and an agreement to divorce in the future. It can also record an agreement about arrangements for any children during the period of separation, and afterwards on divorce. It can also record an agreement about financial arrangements during the separation and upon divorce.

Judicial Separation

If court proceedings are necessary, you can apply for a 'judicial separation'. For example, a judicial separation may be required if you have not yet been married for a year, or if one or both of you have religious objections to divorce.

A judicial separation is a similar process to divorce. You can obtain all the financial orders that you would upon divorce, with the exception of a clean financial break.

In judicial separation proceedings , applications to the court can be made in relation to the children. If there are no proceedings, stand-alone applications can still be made in relation to the children under the Children Act 1989. Financial and children orders are both covered in more detail elsewhere in this book.

Dear Marilyn

My husband left me twelve months ago. Since then he has continued to pay for everything in the house and pays me a housekeeping allowance. He has a stressful job and he told me that he needs time to think about life. I'm happy enough and my routine continues, but I miss him dreadfully.

My children believe he has a girlfriend and is "stringing me along". They keep telling me to see a lawyer but it's all right for them. They haven't been married for 30 years and I'm 57 years old. I had been looking forward to my husband's retirement – we had planned to travel and have fun together. Perhaps we still can.

What do you advise?

Sandra

Dear Sandra

Yours is a letter I dread. I think you know the truth, but you won't face it.

You need to talk to him and ask him outright if he does intend to return. Tell him how agonising it is waiting for him, spending lonely days in limbo.

There may be a happy outcome, but personally I think that if people want to be with one another, they will be and nothing will stop them.

None of us can choose what happens in life. Life is a lottery. It has its ups and downs and none of us get a smooth ride. Things don't always work out as we planned. If these worst fears are confirmed, take your own life in hand. Stop wasting your time and start to plan your own future. There is nothing to stop you travelling with friends or family who are acting in your best interests.

Life goes on, and I wish you all the best.

Marilyn

Part II: Getting Divorced

7: The Six Steps to Divorce

Dear Marilyn

This isn't going to be one of those guides that make divorce sound like a walk in the park, is it? I had expectations about what my own divorce would be like, but I was utterly unprepared for what became a slow, bewildering and miserable experience. It lasted longer than a year and was far more expensive than I had anticipated. I can't help thinking that it could have been settled on day one. Now my children have been turned against me and, when I do see them, all they want is money.

Lee

Dear Lee,

I am very sorry to hear about your experiences. Divorce can be "easy" and straightforward – but that doesn't mean that it will be. I tell my clients that a divorce is like having an operation on top of the Big Dipper, without an anaesthetic. If you know that from the beginning, you are prepared for the worst. If the experience isn't as bad as you had feared, good for you!

Here at Stowe Family Law, all clients are given a booklet that details the various steps, processes and procedures to expect. We also give a realistic estimate of what the costs will be in each case. It is fair to say that overall, most divorces will take between nine and 12 months to resolve, including arrangements for the children and a financial settlement. However in large cities, particularly London, it can take longer because of pressure on court time.

Are there any ways to divorce and avoid court as much as possible? I discuss this in more detail later but in my experience, the quickest cases are those in which I have mediated for both parties. In these cases the parties do know what they want, they both know what their finances are and both are happy to instruct me to help them come to an overall agreement. We draw up this agreement, which they then take to other solicitors for independent ratification and court orders to be made. Such cases can take just two or three months from start to finish. They are very satisfying because neither party has lost control; together, they have reached an agreement. Not all mediators are lawyers: independent mediators can also help couples to reach agreement about finances and children. In general, however, mediation is not a popular option. Perhaps this is because at the outset, most parties do not trust each other and are too emotional. As the case goes on, mediation may seem more of a sensible option. Another option is collaborative law, whereby the parties and their lawyers work amicably around a table to try and resolve the case. If court proceedings become necessary, those lawyers withdraw.

Finally, there is the newest option: family law arbitration. Parties present cases to a qualified arbitrator, who adjudicates their case and makes a legally binding decision. I explain all these options in more detail in **Chapter eight: What To Do Before You Do Anything Else.** At Stowe Family Law we offer all these options to our clients, but in my experience, most clients opt for the "traditional" route because they prefer the outcome to be ordered by a judge, if necessary. This has been the case since I first became a mediator back in the mid-1990s. Perhaps times will change.

Overall, you are right: the emotional fallout of a divorce, however it is tackled and however it turns out, can be difficult to deal with. Your relationship with your former spouse may improve or it may not. And what about children? Children see things differently to parents. Younger children are especially vulnerable. Be the best parent that you can be. What comforts do your children need? How can you reassure them that what has happened is not their fault? Encourage your children to acclimatise,

*and to participate in your new lifestyle as you are
participating in theirs. Let time heal.*

Marilyn

Let's begin with the basics. I must admit that I am not a big fan of lists such as these, although I often see them popping up in other books and on the internet. To my mind, they can create an impression that relationship breakdown is a simple process: 'divorce-by-numbers', if you will.

I accept that some cases really are as straightforward as they are intended to be in theory and in the eyes of the law. However, divorces and splits are often messy and fraught with unexpected complications. I have had clients who found out that they were not legally married after all, clients whose spouses died unexpectedly before proceedings were completed and clients who discovered that were entitled to far more than they had thought. None of us can know what lies around the corner, just out of sight.

So think of these lists as the pencil sketches of a break-up or divorce. The chapters that follow will provide the colour, paint and texture.

A Note on Civil Partnerships

When couples in same sex civil partnerships break up, they do not "divorce"; instead, their relationship is "dissolved". However, the legal steps are almost identical to divorce: what is written here about divorce, unless specifically excluded, applies to civil partnerships in equal measure.

Divorce

In England and Wales, divorce is currently granted on the basis of a single ground: the irretrievable breakdown of marriage. One of five "facts" can be used to prove that "irretrievable breakdown" has taken place. They are:

• Adultery. (This is not a basis for obtaining a dissolution of a civil partnership, because the definition of adultery is that consensual sexual intercourse has taken place between a man and woman, one or both of whom are married.)

• Unreasonable behaviour.

• Desertion for a period of two years or more.

• Two years' separation with consent.

• Five years' separation without consent.

The majority of divorces take place with unreasonable behaviour or adultery cited. They offer a relatively speedy route to divorce. When a marriage breaks down it is not too difficult to alight upon instances of unreasonable behaviour.

It is important at the outset to understand that in the vast majority of cases, the reason given for divorce has no impact upon financial settlements, questions of residence or contact with the children of the marriage. The general ethos is to end a marriage with dignity. There have been calls to simplify the divorce process, remove fault and turn it into an administrative rather than judicial process.

1. **As of now, divorce remains a six-step process:-**The first step is to lodge the divorce petition with the court. If there are children to the marriage, the petition must be accompanied by a Statement of the Arrangements for Children. The court will then send a

copy of the petition to the other partner. The partner who lodges the petition is the petitioner; the other partner is the respondent. If the reason for the divorce is adultery and a third person is named in the petition, he or she is called the co-respondent. You cannot lodge a divorce petition until you have been married for at least a year. A note on co-respondents: even if you have the opportunity to name a co-respondent on your divorce petition, I do not recommend that you do so. Such naming is not necessary; a decision to "name and shame" may therefore come across as embittered and vengeful. It is unlikely to impress a judge because it adds to the costs and causes unnecessary conflict. My advice is to save your powder for dealing with the children and finances.

2. **The respondent must complete an Acknowledgement of Service document and indicate any intention to defend the divorce.** (The majority of divorces in this country are undefended. If you defend the divorce, you may end up having to pay the costs of a prolonged and bitter battle . In 30 years, I have only had to deal with one defended divorce. In that case the other party, who opposed our client's petition, ended up paying the costs.) He or she has seven days to reply and should consult a solicitor at this stage.

3. **The Acknowledgement of Service is returned to the court, which sends a copy to the petitioner or their lawyer.** The petitioner's next step is to file an affidavit, confirming that the details of the divorce petition are correct. Once the affidavit is sworn it is re-

turned to the court.

4. **The affidavit is placed before a district judge.** If the judge decides that the documentation is in order, a certificate is granted and sent to the petitioner, giving a date when the decree nisi will be pronounced in court. (Note: in the case of a civil partnership, the decree nisi is replaced by a conditional order.)

5. **On the specified date, the decree nisi is pronounced in court.** It is not necessary for anyone to be in court on this occasion. It is important to recognise that the decree nisi does not end the marriage. Partners cannot remarry until the decree absolute has been obtained. (Note: in the case of a civil partnership, the decree absolute is replaced by a final order.) Financially speaking, the decree nisi is an important stage, because the court has power to make a final order at this point.

6. **Six weeks after the decree nisi is issued, the petitioner can apply for the decree to be made absolute.** A sealed copy of the decree absolute is sent to both parties and this should be produced as evidence of divorce on remarriage. If the petitioner delays applying for the decree absolute, a respondent may apply three months after the earliest date that the petitioner could have applied for it. At this point a financial order can be implemented.

In theory the procedure is straightforward and basic, with a divorce taking around 12 to 16 weeks from start to finish. In theory are the words that I'd like to emphasise here. The decree absolute has unexpectedly proved to be the thorniest topic on my blog. I have had hundreds of queries from people who don't know whether or not to apply for the decree absolute, because they know it will end their marriage and they are not sure if it will affect their financial position. In most cases the decree absolute will make no difference, but in a few cases, there can be good reasons to delay applying for it. For example, to protect your rights and benefits in the event of death before a final order is made. Or if there are substantial pension benefits that would automatically be lost in the event of a death before a financial order is made, or if there is a religious divorce going on at the same time in order to ensure that the parties are divorced in religious and civil law together. (This can be particularly important for Jewish or Muslim couples.) Similarly, for wealthier couples who do not yet have a financial settlement in place, it may make sense to wait because benefits received through a trust or company could be lost if the spouse is divorced.

It is important that you and your lawyer, if you instruct one, discuss the best time for you to be finally divorced. Remember that once divorced you cannot become a widow or widower. Therefore in the unlikely but still possible event of a spouse's death before the decree absolute, you would not be entitled to any widow's or widower's automatic entitlements on death.

Civil partners obtain Conditional and Final Orders for dissolution of a civil partnership.

A small but very important point: once divorced, if you haven't yet applied for a financial settlement, please don't remarry without telling your solicitor first! You could lose out on your divorce settlement.

Cohabiting couples

If you have been living together and the relationship breaks down, your legal rights are relatively limited. Your entitlement to tax credits and benefits may change. However, the law does not make provision for one cohabitant to claim maintenance from the other. (If there are children and one partner is wealthy, a "carer's allowance" may be granted.) Cohabitants' rights to the family home and any other property are not always straightforward.

1. **If you possess a "Living Together Agreement" in the form of a signed deed,** which sets out what you both promised to do if the relationship ended, it is legally enforceable.

2. **If you do not possess such an agreement,** your recourse to the law is restricted. However you may go to court to resolve any ownership disputes over property and any disputes over child maintenance. In the midst of separation, a cohabiting couple experiences the same emotional turmoil as a married couple going through a divorce. I see increasing numbers of unmarried clients in my offices, and I have very strong feelings about the lack of suitable legislation for them. Although much of this book applies to cohabiting couples, married couples and civil partners alike, chapter 12 has been written with cohabiting couples in mind and covers legal rights in greater detail.

8: What to Do Before You Do Anything Else

So you have weighed up the situation, assessed the pros and cons and made the decision to divorce. Congratulations: you have taken control of the situation and taken the first step on the road to the rest of your life. Now what?

This is likely to be one of the most critical periods – if not the most critical period – of the divorce process. The decision-making isn't over yet. The choices you make now are likely to have a significant impact upon the emotional and financial outcomes.

The first decisions

1. **Choose a good solicitor, if you can afford one.** You must decide upon the lawyer who will represent you and steer your case to its conclusion. Your decision is important: your solicitor can make or break your case.

2. **Consider the various methods of divorce and the associated costs.** Your choice must also be agreed with your spouse. Options on offer include "DIY divorce", mediation, collaborative divorce and family law arbitration, in additional to "regular", lawyer-assisted divorce.

3. **Consider your financial needs and your children's financial needs.** What urgent assistance do you require? How are you going to manage financially until a full financial settlement has been implemented? Immediate needs are called "interim" by lawyers. You must also consider the following questions: what assets

do you need to protect? Is there any ongoing financial haemorrhage that must be dealt with? A credit card that needs to be stopped? A bank account that should be frozen? You need to think fast but please, don't panic. It's rare for anything to go wrong that cannot be put right. Even if your wealthy spouse walks out leaving you with nothing, you may get a small overdraft from the bank, or borrow on credit cards or make an immediate application to the court for interim maintenance. Your solicitor should be able to advise further and again, I would suggest you find a good family lawyer who offers a free first interview. Many do, so don't assume they won't. When I sit down with a new client for the first time, I consider how best to protect them. For example, what about assets held in one name only? How is the asset to be protected? It is possible to register a charge at the Land Registry in relation to property owned solely in the name of the other spouse, if you have proceedings underway. In more complicated situations it is sometimes necessary to apply for an injunction, not only to protect assets but also to obtain documents or computers that might help you obtain a clear financial picture if your spouse is devious. Again, these are extreme situations, which usually only arise when more sensible avenues have been exhausted. But think carefully about your situation and what you know about the finances. If immediate action is required to stabilise your position, take it. Prevent losses from mounting and monies from being dissipated to your disadvantage.

4. **Keep what you have.** If there is a significant sum

lying in a joint bank account, you will have to consider
what to do with it. The least controversial option is simply to freeze the account. It may not be a good idea to
divide it up, because not all assets will be divided equally and you may be agreeing to divide an asset that will
later come to you in its entirety. I will ask my client to
write to the bank, asking the bank manager to refuse to
pay any money out in the absence of joint signatures.
If other assets are held in joint names, such as stocks
and shares, I will ask my client to write to the broker in
similar terms. If there is a drawdown mortgage, I will
ask my client to write to the building society, to ensure
that my client's written consent is obtained before any
future drawdowns are made. It is essential to take steps
to preserve the status quo, but it is also essential to take
steps that leave you with the ability to manage your finances during this interim period until a full financial
settlement has been negotiated. This will include monies for the children too; the payment of school fees is a
frequent source of argument, and I would suggest that
school fees are paid out of income rather than capital.
More likely than not, the capital will be required to pay
for two houses.

Some changes to the law that you should know about

Family law changes fast. Since 1973 there have been some
momentous developments. This quick guide should bring you
up to date and push aside any redundant ideas and mistaken
assumptions sooner, rather than later.

Some of the changes are as follows:

1. **Wives do receive larger payouts.** The balance of financial settlements has altered since 2000 with the momentous case of White v White, the impact of which continues and has been covered substantially on my blog. It is now recognised that a non-working wife contributes as much to her marriage as her working husband does. If you are the breadwinner, do not make the mistake of thinking that all monies are "yours", with your spouse entitled to money only at your discretion.

2. **Courts are more likely to enforce foreign judgments.** Increasingly our courts show they are acting in tandem with foreign courts, particularly those in Europe, to discourage "forum shopping" by parties who are looking for the "best" court to hear their case and therefore obtain the most favourable settlement. Likewise, abroad it is becoming easier to enforce judgments which have been made in our jurisdiction.

3. **Prenuptial agreements are receiving increased recognition.** English law does not automatically recognise such agreements, (although it soon will when the law changes in the next couple of years), but at the time of writing it will now uphold them if certain conditions have been met. These include meeting the other party's needs.

4. **Journalists have access to family courts.** We had one instance in which an embittered spouse, who wished to embarrass our client, invited a journalist to attend a court hearing. Presumably the spouse hoped that the journalist would report on the case. The jour-

nalist did attend – but was so bored by the proceedings that he did not bother showing up on the second day, when the judgment was given. The press may attend hearings, but the judge will only give them permission to report details of the case in exceptional circumstances. The real risk of embarrassment comes with a decision by a high court judge to report his or her judgment so the parties can be identified. And the parties will be fully identified, as will their case, if it is heard by the Court of Appeal.

5. **Courts are increasingly sympathetic towards fathers.** *See chapter 24: What's the Deal with Dad?* for further details.

6. **Family law remains a movable feast.** And how! Bear in mind that at the time of writing, the entire law of divorce, both process and financial may yet change before our eyes. In recent years, key judgments have drastically altered the family law landscape, for example in relation to the division of assets. Reform of the law relating to cohabiting couples, meanwhile, has been keenly anticipated but has not yet taken place. Try to follow these developments, as they may affect you. My blog, www.marilynstowe.co.uk, will help to keep you fully updated.

Choosing the right divorce for you

Dear Marilyn

My husband and I have concluded, with regret, that our marriage is over. We would like to remain friends – this is a priority for us. We can both afford to pay for lawyers, but is it ever possible to stay on good terms, if lawyers become involved?

Jo

Dear Jo,

The answer is yes, why not? Lawyers can only advise; you instruct your lawyer. You and your husband are the ones issuing the proceedings and setting the pace. If your solicitor proposes a plan of action that makes you feel uncomfortable, you should tell him or her immediately.

I have known many clients to remain on good terms with their former partners. That is down to them, not their lawyers. However mediation, teamed with sound professional advice, does appear to provide a good foundation for any future friendship.

Marilyn

Become partners with your lawyer.

Some clients play games. They try the "good cop, bad cop"

approach with their spouse. Their lawyers are the bad guys and they are the good ones. They want strong lawyers to fight for them and protect them. They want their lawyers to take the flak while they try and remain on reasonable terms with their partners. Some lawyers are aware of this from the outset. Others are not.

I read in the press that family lawyers can inflame and prolong the divorce process. Perhaps some do, but I am more sceptical. Clients can and do play games, usually because they feel weak and out of control. It is easy to blame the lawyers if something does not go right.

My advice to clients is to take control, but as part of a partnership with the lawyer. My own clients know from the outset what is likely to happen in their own cases, because my years of experience mean that I can advise my clients fearlessly and predict the likely outcomes with confidence. I can therefore advise them how to take their case forward.

A number of my clients do wish to negotiate directly with their spouses. I don't have a problem with this at all, provided that negotiations are not rushed, take place on an equal footing and with both parties fully informed about assets. Sadly, it is a fact of life that some people will try to take advantage of vulnerable partners - and not every client appreciates that he or she is not as competent at negotiating as their spouse is. They think they know it all, and attempt to negotiate a financial settlement that may have to last the rest of their lifetime. I cannot sufficiently emphasise how important this task is. It is the key to your future and so it must, repeat must, be carried out correctly. There is little chance of going back on a financial settlement that has been approved by the court.

More recently, other services have been introduced and have been gaining popularity. These include mediation , collaborative law and family law arbitration. These have their advantages and disadvantages, in terms of cost, speed, effectiveness and outcomes, and you are advised to discuss each option with your solicitor before making your decision. This primer should assist you with that decision; my unequivocal advice is that if it is possible for you to negotiate a deal commercially, you should do it.

'DIY' Divorce

Pros

- Straightforward and cost-effective. A couple with no financial problems, who are in agreement, can certainly obtain a divorce without the assistance of a solicitor. They can go along to court, or obtain the forms online and get going.
- It is possible to instruct a lawyer for "hand-holding", to reduce costs. Consult a solicitor only when you need to do so, and do the rest of the work yourself. This will work out much cheaper but you will still have professional support if you need it.

Cons

- If you take no legal advice at all, gaping financial pitfalls can result. You are entitled to agree to demands that place you at a financial disadvantage – but you may come to regret these down the line. Or you may agree to demands only to discover, sometime later, that you were "bilked" of your rights and entitlements. For these reasons, again, legal advice is recommended.

- The form-filling and legalese are not for everyone. Doing your own divorce has been compared to doing the conveyancing for your own house.
- If you choose this method, you can obtain forms from your local county court. Alternatively you can download them from www.courtservice.gov.uk. Remember that the Citizens Advice Bureau may be able to assist with queries and individual advice.

Collaborative divorce

Pros

- This concept has gained popularity. It involves the spouses and their lawyers sitting at a "negotiating table" in a series of four-way meetings, discussing the important issues. For example: if the house should be sold; how the proceeds of sale should be divided; where the children will live and on what days, and what the various options for resolving those issues might be. The aim: to agree a fair outcome for both parties and thrash out a deal without the need to go to court.
- It allows a more "holistic" approach towards a family breakdown, by introducing other specialists such as financial advisers who are specially trained to give impartial advice on how best to divide investments and pensions, or who can advise on the costs of borrowing for future mortgages.

Cons

- No guarantee of success. Furthermore, if the parties cannot reach agreement and the process fails, both spouses must change their lawyers.

- The costs vary from case to case. The legal fees can be relatively low, because this method of divorce keeps the couple out of court. However, with lawyers charging by the hour, fees can begin to mount if the negotiating process becomes prolonged.
- We have been offering collaborative divorces at Stowe Family Law since 2007. You can also find a trained collaborative lawyer by contacting Resolution: its details are listed in the _Useful Resources_ section at the back of this book.

Mediation

Pros

- It is the most "civilised" method of divorce. A couple sits down with a professional, independent mediator (who may or may not be legally qualified) to discuss and agree how their finances, property and children are to be dealt with. Their lawyers can participate in the process, if the clients wish it.
- Speed. If you are prepared to give and take, this is probably the fastest method of divorce. Disputes can be resolved in just a few weeks. So this method can also be extremely cost-effective.
- Confidentiality. Discussions that take place during mediation remain private.

Cons

- No guarantee of success, particularly if there is any kind of power imbalance such as one spouse fearing the other, or one spouse having more financial knowledge than the other. The power imbalance is corrected if both sides are represented by lawyers who can "cut to the chase" much faster and advise their clients what a court is likely to do.

• It has no "teeth". For example, a court order cannot be obtained to obtain disclosure.

• Mediation presumes that both spouses have "equality of arms" and that they are both sensible, positive and fair-minded. That isn't necessarily the case.

• If the process fails, a delay in settlement is likely to result.

• Less than a third of couples currently see mediation through to its conclusion. This is probably because the mediation process takes place too early, when the parties are not yet ready to compromise and deal directly with one another.

In my experience, when I mention the option of mediation to my clients the answer is usually no. Their view: they have come to me to sort out their divorce and they don't want to involve somebody else. It is very rare for a couple to reach a mutually amicable decision to split, and what the fine theories about mediation do not take into account is the emotional fallout of the situation. Inevitably there are going to be arguments about money, houses and children. By the time the client is sitting in front of me, they are almost beyond having reasonable discussions with their partner. They just want it over. They have lost confidence in themselves, they are nervous and don't feel qualified to sort it all out. That's why they depend on their lawyer.

I have also found that if just one partner shows interest in mediation, it is often the dominant one in the relationship. This person may think that if they can get the spouse on their own, they can talk them round to a settlement on their terms.

I fear that by the time a client decides that things are so bad he or she needs to see me, or any of the other divorce lawyers in the country, then "mediation" may be the last word they want to hear.

In my experience mediation is likely to fail if offered too early, before the couple is ready to talk meaningfully to one another. However I believe mediation can work extremely well when the parties are willing to talk to one another, all the assets are disclosed and both parties have a reasonable idea of their own financial requirements for the future.

I have already described how successful mediation can provide a foundation for a good, platonic relationship between former partners. I have also described how I have successfully mediated clients' cases before now. I do believe that if you choose this option, it is most likely to succeed if it takes place at the right time and your mediator is the most experienced divorce lawyer you can find. There are those who argue that knowledge of the law is unnecessary, but I disagree. Successful mediation requires tried and tested people skills, as well as legal expertise.

It was for all these reasons that, in 2010, we launched a partner firm, specialising in family law mediation. Stowe Family Settlements (www.stowefamilylawsettlements.co.uk) is staffed by mediators who are also qualified family lawyers. They are "lawyer mediators". Our lawyer mediators meet with former couples and discuss the likely outcome of the case if it went to court. They help both parties to decide upon the best possible solution, and help to draw up a formal agreement. They also conduct Mediation Information Assessment Meetings, better known as "MIAMs".

A note on MIAMs

In 2011 the Government introduced new regulations, which apply to most people who plan to go to court for parenting disputes or financial issues following the end of a relationship. Couples are required to attend a 'Mediation Information Assessment Meeting' (MIAM) in order to discuss the benefits and decide whether or not mediation would be appropriate to their situation.

There are exceptions. MIAMS are not required where:

• Both parties are already in agreement.
• No notice of court action has been given to the other person involved.
• There has been an allegation of domestic violence, and there has been a police investigation or court proceedings in relation to this.
• One of the parties is bankrupt where the family dispute involves money or financial issues.
• The whereabouts of the other person is unknown or they cannot be contacted.
• Court action is urgent, because there is a risk to life, liberty or physical safety; or because the delay caused by a MIAM would cause significant risk to a child or a significant risk of a miscarriage of justice, unreasonable hardship or serious problems in dealing with the dispute (for example, the loss of significant evidence).

- Social services are involved due to child protection concerns or issues.
- A child would be a participant in the possible court proceedings.
- The person planning the court action or their legal representative has contacted three family mediators within 15 miles of the person's home and none have been available to conduct a MIAM within 15 days of being contacted.

I have great reservations about the Government's current determination to push family mediation. It knows how badly overcrowded are the courts have become and how overworked most judges now are. Now that legal aid for family law has effectively been abolished, the Government is pushing people into mediation as a cheap stopgap. However mediation is not and cannot be a complete solution to current overcrowding issues. It is a sticking plaster on a gaping wound. The courts offer certainty; mediation does not.

Another concern of mine is that a couple is required to attend a MIAM before the parties are required to make full and frank disclosure of their finances. If you decide to pursue mediation and your spouse is less than honest about his or her financial situation, you may be placed at a disadvantage.

At the time of writing, the current requirement to attend a MIAM is not rigorously enforced. Your solicitor, if you have one, can advise you further, but please note that MIAMs have been introduced relatively recently and the requirements relating to them may change in the future.

Family Law Arbitration

Qualified arbitrators can now decide a range of financial family law issues with legally binding outcomes or "awards". I am one of the first family law arbitrators in England and Wales to qualify under the new scheme.

The family law arbitration scheme covers financial and property disputes arising from family relationship; including divorce settlements, financial provision for children, property and inheritance issues.

The process is straightforward: after both agreeing to undertake arbitration, disputing parties can nominate an arbitrator or have one assigned by the Institute of Family Law Arbitrators. Parties then present cases to the arbitrator, who adjudicates their case and, ultimately, makes a legally binding decision.

I believe it is particularly well-suited to two groups of people: those in big money cases who can circumvent the waiting period in the courts and also are prepared to pay the fees of the arbitrator to have the benefit of privacy, and litigants who might want an arbitrator to decide the case or a specific point. Arbitration is tailored to the couple and we do not have to go through the entire process which we do in court. If you do not need a hearing, the arbitrator can decide something on paper. It's more informal and quicker.

Pros

- Speed. Subject to the arbitrator's availability, the timetable is up to the parties to agree. This is in marked contrast to court procedures, and in nearly all cases is likely to be significantly faster.

- Confidentiality. The entire process is confidential by its nature.
- Costs. In many cases, there may be a saving of overall costs over court proceedings. The parties have to pay the arbitrator's fees, the cost of any venue which is hired, and the cost of a transcription service, if required. However the ability to limit disclosure and the ambit of the dispute, if properly utilised by the parties, should in many cases lead to a net cost saving.
- Flexibility. It will be for the parties to define the scope of the arbitration. In many cases they will want all their differences arbitrated. In others the arbitration could be limited to discrete issues. It is also possible for an arbitration to be completed on paper, if the parties agree or the arbitrator so directs. There may be flexibility as to the time and place of hearings.
- Choice of arbitrator. Parties to a dispute never have the right to choose which Judge will try their case in court, but they do have the right under the Scheme to choose their arbitrator. Knowing that a dispute will be resolved by a selected specialist with appropriate experience will be very attractive to many parties and their advisers. The same arbitrator deals with all stages of the case from start to finish.

Cons

- Once the parties have agreed to the arbitration, the arbitrator must deliver the award unless both parties agree to end the process.
- Because family law arbitration is so new, there remain

some issues as to how effectively an award can be enforced. However enforcement in a court process is sometimes a problem too.

Lawyer-assisted divorce

Pros

- A good lawyer will have the confidence and commercial awareness to help you make important decisions about your future and the future of your family. In cases where there are major assets and major decisions to be made, it doesn't make sense to DIY.
- A good lawyer will also help you rebuild your life. Many clients have suffered from a loss of confidence at the hands of their spouses. As well as ending the marriage, a client needs to be able to re-establish himself or herself in a new life.
- Some clients are wracked with guilt when they divorce. I tell them that none of us are perfect. You aren't on trial for a criminal offence. Lawyers aren't therapists, but divorce is an emotionally turbulent time, during which you will benefit from as much peace of mind and support as you can get. A good lawyer can provide this.

Cons

- The process can be daunting and you need to keep in your mind that you are instructing the lawyer rather than the other way round. Never be afraid to remind your lawyer of any concerns you may have, given that you are paying the bill. If you are paying for "hand-holding" only, it is particularly important to keep a grip on costs.

- The litigation route can be costly and time-consuming. Your lawyer will send you a retainer letter, even if acting entirely pro bono (free of charge). Please read it. Keep your eye on the ball at all times. Ask yourself, *"Is it necessary to send this letter to the other side?"* - especially if it is to complain about something that your lawyer has already advised is trivial. Normally you will be charged by your lawyer for each letter, phone call, meeting and court attendance. Remember that, particularly when you are burning up with anger over your spouse. Many clients try to turn their cases into games of ping pong. Don't do it. Don't be the client who thinks money is no object until the case is over - and then bitterly regrets it.

CASEBOOK

Be pragmatic. An early settlement can often seem like a simple, easy way out - but it isn't always the right answer. I recall one lady who came to discuss a four-page draft agreement from her husband's solicitor. She was calm and confident when she arrived, but when I went through the agreement with her, clause by clause, she became angry and upset as the awful truth dawned. In simple terms, she was being conned. Several months later the settlement had been properly concluded, and our client's interests had been fully protected.

Another client, who was seriously ill at the time, was prevailed upon by her unscrupulous husband

> *to put her signature to a grossly unfair "agree-*
> *ment". He then fought to uphold this "agreement"*
> *through the courts. He was unsuccessful, and his*
> *efforts cost him an additional £500,000 plus both*
> *parties' costs. Since then, that man has referred a*
> *fair few clients to me!*

Cases such as these demonstrate the value of good legal representation working in partnership with the client. Divorce is emotionally turbulent, and the support provided by an effective legal team should not be under-estimated. That is what family lawyers are paid for.

9: How to Choose a Good Solicitor

Your next step should be to instruct a solicitor, if you can do so, even if it is only for "hand-holding".

At times like this, when your emotions are in turmoil, this search can be an additional, unwanted burden. Where do you start? What should you look for in a solicitor? How can you tell a good lawyer from a mediocre one?

I hope that the following checklists will make it easy and simple for you to make the best possible choice.

Checklist: the signs of a good family solicitor

1. **The solicitor enjoys an excellent word-of-mouth reputation.** When you are looking for a solicitor, ask for pointers from friends and relatives who have been through the divorce process themselves. They usually have the inside track on the good, the bad and the ugly. Many of my clients are referred to me by former clients and far more, by people I have acted against!

2. **The solicitor has a green and black Law Society - Family Law, or Law Society – Advanced logo outside their office or on their stationery.** This distinctive logo, which features two adults and a child, is used under licence from the Law Society's Family Law Panel. It is your assurance that the lawyer using it has been judged by their peers to be a competent and caring professional. If they hold an Advanced logo,they have reached an even higher standard in certain aspects of family law. The Law Society is the governing body for

solicitors. It created the Family Law Panel to recognise good family lawyers. Only those solicitors who have passed a rigorous test of professional ability can use the logo. I can vouch for the quality of this accreditation: I was appointed the Family Law Panel's first Chief Examiner and Chief Assessor. The question we asked ourselves, when assessing candidates, was: *"Would we be happy to recommend them to a friend or relative who was about to go through a divorce?"* Family lawyers in this country adhere to high professional standards, and the work of the Family Law Panel is helping to raise those standards higher still.

3. **The solicitor will be able to give a good steer at the very first meeting**, having extracted all the relevant information about the client and the factors that a court will take into account. The solicitor should be able to provide details of outcomes in similar cases and the likely outcome in your case. I'm not a fortune teller, but I can advise about what is likely to happen in most cases, usually with the parameters within which I think the court will make its decision. Even in the most complicated cases, with the most complicated of assets, it is possible to advise a client about the likely outcome of a split. I will also provide an estimate of the likely costs of the case. This is advice that clients need to know - however difficult it is to give.

4. **The solicitor is caring and compassionate, but doesn't tiptoe around you.** If there are likely obstacles, or if you are chasing impossible dreams, a good divorce solicitor will inform you immediately. They will

be frank and direct with you, without appearing unkind or uncaring. Counselling is an important part of a solicitor's job, as is full discussion of the likelihood of reconciliation.

5. **The solicitor is straightforward and knowledgeable.** A good lawyer has a straightforward manner and does not fill you with false hope. They aren't afraid to discuss how much it is all going to cost. They know what they are talking about, and you come away feeling confident.

Dear Marilyn

I first contacted my divorce solicitor after seeing an ad for her firm in the paper, but now I am worried that I have chosen poorly. We have had only one meeting so far, but I wasn't impressed. I felt uncomfortable in her presence, although I couldn't tell you why. Does that sound silly? Also, it seems to take an age for her to respond to my telephone messages and emails. My divorce petition has now been lodged with the court; would it be more trouble than it is worth to find a new solicitor for my case?

Nicky

Dear Nicky,

I know exactly how you feel. Two years ago I had

to instruct a solicitor to act for me, on a non-family law matter. When I walked through the door and noticed his firm's uniformed concierges and stainless steel glass lifts, I saw that the place was steeped in affluence. I wondered how much of this I would be paying for. My concerns were exacerbated an hour into my appointment when the lawyer, clearly wanting to get away for lunch, began glancing at his watch! He also told me how busy he was with a major client - and he wasn't referring to me.

When I left his office I felt anxious. My fears, anxieties and worries had not been soothed. I had paid a small fortune for his time, yet had received little concrete advice and had instead been left bewildered. Why hadn't the lawyer taken my worries on his shoulders and endeavoured to let me walk out of his office feeling lighter and reassured? That is what I try and do with all my clients. I decided to give this man the boot and am jolly glad I did.

As a solicitor myself, I cannot expect to hit it off with every client. No solicitor can: it's a matter of personal chemistry. And remember: your solicitor is not a mind reader. He or she cannot guess your concerns if you do not express them, either in person or in writing. However if this lawyer is not right for you, you should take action as soon as possible, before proceedings are under way. Don't be afraid to listen to your instincts.

Marilyn

Checklist: the signs of a 'mediocre' family solicitor

1. **The solicitor glances at the clock throughout your appointment.** A good solicitor will care deeply about your case and will give it their all. They will listen to you. A self-important solicitor who regards you as a fixed - and not altogether welcome - unit of activity is unlikely to do the same.

2. **The solicitor fobs you off when you enquire about costs.** You will want to know about likely outcomes and costs, and you will want reassurance. If a solicitor cannot provide this advice, even when it is qualified within a range of parameters, I don't think that this person should be advising you. In truth, I don't understand why some solicitors do not advise their clients about financial proceedings as soon as they can. If the solicitor is acting in the client's best interests and it isn't one of those exceptional cases in which the parties are in close agreement, this should be a no-brainer. The court doesn't regard it as an aggressive stance, it keeps costs contained and it timetables the case so that the end is in sight.

3. **The solicitor insists upon "voluntary disclosure" of assets as the way forward.** They will believe - usually wrongly, in my opinion - that it will preserve good relations between the parties. I disagree in most cases. Voluntary disclosure has no "teeth" and shifts power away from the client; a party refusing to play ball, who wishes to drag out negotiations, need not produce full disclosure because there is no court sanc-

tion. On occasion, some solicitors are even prepared to advise clients on the basis of disclosure that is unsworn and therefore, in my view, should not be relied upon. It means that if and when negotiations break down, the entire process - or most of it - will have to begin again, under the auspices of the court. Costs will climb. Be warned!

4. **The solicitor is arrogant and does not listen to you.** Solicitors charge high rates and you want to feel that you are getting value for money. If your solicitor is always flustered and waffles non-stop, what does that tell you? If you spend an hour with them and come away none the wiser about your case, it doesn't bode well. If your solicitor doesn't clearly explain the options, ask you to think about what you want, how you see your future, where you are going to live, and discuss it with you, then don't blame him or her if, after the case is over, you aren't happy. You need to say so. Sometimes, what you want isn't what the lawyer would advise. But if your mind is made up, say so. If you don't have that type of relationship with your solicitor, he or she isn't the right one for you.

CASEBOOK

Mr D came to see me because he wanted a second opinion about his divorce case. He had instructed a local solicitor, who charged little but brimmed with confidence. The solicitor had assured Mr D that family law was straightforward.

A few months down the line, Mr D's case had made little progress. Whenever he asked his solicitor about financial considerations he was told, "Let's look at a settlement when we know the whole picture". The situation dragged on, and costs mounted. Mr D was having sleepless nights and feared there would be nothing left after his wife - whose solicitor certainly knew what he was doing - had finished with him.

I have noticed that solicitors who do not specialise in family law can be inclined to think that it is a relatively easy field to conquer. In truth, family law is much more complex than it may appear to be at first.

When I read the case correspondence, I was alarmed. The couple's assets were complicated and Mr D's fears were well-founded. His wife's solicitors had taken advantage of the other solicitor's inexperience and were calling all the shots. My firm took on Mr D's case; we were able to turn it around and settle the case fairly. For the client it was a close call.

Checklist: What to take to the first appointment

This isn't an exhaustive list, but the information will be helpful to your solicitor, especially if you are nervous and become forgetful. It will also save time at your first meeting. It is a good idea to send this information a few days before your appointment, if possible, so that your lawyer has had time to study it in advance.

- Your original marriage (or civil partnership) certificate.
- Any letters to or from the CSA.
- Copies of any court orders concerning your marriage or your children.
- Any letters from your partner's solicitor.

On a separate piece of A4 paper:
- Your full name and date of birth.
- Your occupation.
- Your telephone numbers and e-mail address.
- Your residential address.
- A "safe" correspondence address. This is an address (usually a friend's or a family member's) at which mail addressed to you cannot be intercepted by your partner or an unwanted third party.
- A "safe" e-mail address, at which mail addressed to you cannot be intercepted by your partner or an unwanted third party. It is also important that your password for this e-mail account is almost impossible to guess.
- A "safe" telephone number. It is unusual for partners to bug telephones, but it does happen. For this reason we recommend that clients contact us using pay-as-you-go mobile phones. The phone number should not be shared with others.
- Your National Insurance number.
- Your partner's full name and date of birth.
- Your partner's occupation.

- Your partner's address (if your partner no longer lives with you).
- Date of any separation.
- Dates of any previous marriage(s) entered into by you or your partner, together with dates of any final decrees.
- Your children's full names and dates of birth.
- Names and addresses of your children's school(s).
- Names, dates of birth and names of parents of any children who are members of the household but are not children of you both.
- Two forms of ID. These can include the original of your passport, driving licence and utility bills. These will be needed to prove your identity and address, to comply with your solicitor's money laundering procedure.

Details of your case

Use the following as a guide and compile information as appropriate:

- Brief details of the nature of your problem.
- Your income and your partner's income. (Don't worry if, at this stage, it is only round figures or an estimate.)
- Details of properties: addresses, ownership, amounts outstanding on any mortgages, types of mortgage (such as ordinary repayment, endowment or pension linked).
- Approximate values of any properties. If in doubt, contact a local estate agent for a rough idea. Properties abroad are more difficult to value, but details of the purchase price will help.
- Details of any other assets. These will include money in

banks or building societies, monies invested in shares or insurances, pensions (rough values will help) and all other items such as house contents, cars, furniture, jewellery and antiques. Are there any trusts that you know of? Any offshore assets?

• Details of any companies and shareholdings. Details of business partnerships. Don't worry if you have only a vague idea or none at all. This is common. An experienced solicitor will unearth the position.

• Details of any debts, to whom the debt is owed and how much. These details include guarantees that may have been given to secure borrowings.

• Your thoughts about practical interim arrangements going forward and longer term, if you have been able to think that far ahead. These will include your immediate and longer-term income requirements and housing needs. Don't worry if this is too daunting at first. However a focus upon practical matters, and where and how you would like to live in the future, is an important part of the divorce process. It is examined in more detail later in this book.

Worksheet:
costs questions to ask at the first appointment

The Law Society requires solicitors to inform clients about likely legal costs before the first appointment. Ensure that you are aware of your solicitor's charge-out rate. Do not presume that your first appointment is free, unless this has been confirmed in writing.

Keep this page marked and take your Kindle with you to

your first appointment with your new solicitor. You won't forget any of the questions and if you also take a notebook, you can fill out the answers there and then. Feel free to add any further questions you may have. Your solicitor should send you a note of the meeting immediately afterwards to confirm the advice you have been given, along with a client retainer letter that confirms all the housekeeping information. This note will be an aide memoir.

1. **Please could you provide more detailed information about the likely costs?** *(Note: at the first appointment you should also be asked to sign a form, to confirm that you are aware of the solicitor's charge-out rate for the first meeting.)*
2. **How long is this divorce likely to take?**
3. **Who will be working on my case?** How will my case be supervised?
4. **How often will I be billed?** What are the payment terms?
5. **To whom do I address any complaints about your service or my case?**
6. **How often will I come to your office, and how much of this work can be conducted via e-mail or fax?**
7. **How often will I attend court?**
8. **Is an alternative form of dispute resolution appropriate in my case?**
9. **What about outside assistance?** For example, are barristers, forensic accountants or other experts required?

10. Are my costs recoverable from my spouse?
11. How can I pay my costs as the case progresses,
    if I don't have the money available?

10: Digging In For Divorce

Dear Marilyn

I'm absolutely terrified! My wife and I decided, reluctantly, that divorce was the right thing to do. I'll admit though, that I'm pole axed by the prospect. Part of me is dragging my heels - and the other part of me just wants to get it over and done with as quickly as possible. Now that I have appointed a lawyer, can I just sit back? Or could I be doing more?

James

Dear James,

Be proactive. Ask your solicitor for a copy of Form E, which is a financial disclosure document. Complete it. Begin to give some thought to your income requirements and capital requirements for you and your spouse. Who needs what? What are the assets? Where will you both live? How are you going to share the children? Think carefully about school holidays and festivals such as Christmas and Easter. This is ultimately what divorce comes down to: what you both need, how the assets will be shared out and how you will both manage your children.

I think it is important, if you can, to stay on

> *good terms with your spouse. You may not agree*
> *with one another about budgets and needs, but*
> *you should give these matters some thought sooner*
> *rather than later. Concentrate on divorce's practi-*
> *cal, rather than emotional, aspects.*
>
> *Marilyn*

Conflicting out

This is a rarely glimpsed area of legal practice, but it is one
with which you should familiarise yourself, just in case. Es-
sentially a "conflict" applies to a situation in which it is inap-
propriate for a solicitor to advise a client, because of previous
or ongoing work with another person involved in the same
case. It can be as straightforward as being instructed by a husband and then being approached by his wife to act in the divorce, but it can also become hugely complicated if partners,
step-families or lovers are involved.

Our firm, like others, keeps a database of clients past and
present so that we can quickly find details of those for whom
we have previously acted. At other times the conflict isn't immediately apparent, or people are not forthcoming with the
required information. When this happens and a conflict is
detected, we often have no choice other than to inform the
second client that we cannot represent them.

Sometimes people make a deliberate attempt to "conflict
out" their spouse's intended solicitor. I have known of some
people who try and conflict out every solicitor in the locality.
I have known of some solicitors who advise their client to con-

flict out another solicitor against whom they would rather not be up against in court. It is a dirty trick but is sadly becoming common.

If this happens to you, check with the lawyer of your choice and do not assume that they are no longer available. If certain criteria have not been met, they may still be able to act for you. At Stowe Family Law, for example, we are quite wise to this now and we have found ways around it!

However if your lawyer has indeed been "conflicted out", don't take it personally. It isn't your fault and it isn't the lawyer's fault. It happens. But please find another lawyer as soon as possible, using the guide from the previous chapter.

CASEBOOK

I saw a new client, "Mr V", who had given a fictitious name and details when arranging his appointment. This happens to us sometimes, usually when the client is well known in the local area or in the media. The conflict check against him came back clear - as one might expect.

When the man began to talk to me, he was in tears. He said that picking up courage to talk to a lawyer about the marriage was deeply painful, but that he had discovered his wife was having an affair. The atmosphere at home was intolerable and he believed her heart was elsewhere. He was consumed by sadness, bitterness, anger and jealousy. He loathed the man who had "stolen" his wife and

---

ended his marriage.

When "Mr V" gave me his real name, I suddenly thought about a client I had seen a few months previously and wondered if there could be a conflict. I asked him the name of the man with whom his wife was having an affair, and he told me.

I recognised the name because a few months earlier, its owner had come to see me. This client was charming and good looking - and he knew it. He was thinking about leaving his wife,wanted to know what the financial consequences would be and took advice as coolly as he would any commercial option.

So I had to do something very unpleasant. I had to tell the heartbroken man sitting in front of me that I was unable to advise him. When he asked why, I confirmed that there was a conflict but I could not say anything else.

"Mr V" knew his wife had seen another solicitor. He guessed that my client must be her lover. At this point he lost his temper. He claimed that the man had stolen his wife and now his lawyer.

I sympathised with his plight, but had he given me his real details at the outset, the conflict situation would not have arisen.

Apart from properly identifying yourself, here are some additional practical tips to help your solicitor get the best for you.

1. **Turn up to appointments on time and allow yourself time to make the most of them.** Solicitors often have busy schedules and may have to cut your appointment short if you are late. When this happens, the person who loses out is you. Equally we might not be able to see you on the dot. Some clients may overrun; others may have an emergency. Please don't glare at the receptionist, tap your foot, cough loudly and pointedly keep consulting your watch. We can't help it!

2. **Be proactive.** This isn't the time or place to feel sorry for yourself and lose control. Obtain all the financial information requested by your lawyer. Don't leave anything out. Obtain details of houses where you might wish to live. Think about how much it is going to cost you and your spouse to run two homes. Make enquiries, prepare a budget and do everything you can to assist your lawyer in terms of being practical. It will reduce your bill.

3. **Don't pester your solicitor unnecessarily.** Several phone calls about the same subject won't help. Neither will a bombardment of emails. Your case is important but it may not be possible for your solicitor to reply by return.

4. **Speak!** If you know what you want, give clear instructions. Don't feel that you dare not speak, then leave consumed with anger and frustration. This is your case, so

have your say.

5. **Don't lose your sense of humour.** This is easier said than done, but pleasant meetings are always more productive.

6. **Avoid alcohol.** Don't drink before an appointment. If you resort to Dutch courage, your solicitor will be able to tell. An addled mind can slow a case's progress.

7. **Do not attend with an entourage in tow.** Do you really need them there, or are they just getting in the way? You don't need sympathy. You do need sensible legal advice.

8. **Don't give instructions against your will or better judgement.** For example, don't tell your solicitor that your spouse can take the children on holiday, when in truth you do not want them to go. You may wish to appear reasonable but if you issue instructions only to change your mind at a later date, you make things more difficult for everyone. If you don't want to take advice, then don't. But don't blame your lawyers if it then goes wrong. The risk is yours.

9. **If you have a problem with your bills of costs then you must say so**. Solicitors and costs go hand in hand. I believe that problems arise when, deep down, clients don't want to pay their lawyers. There are many more pleasant ways to spend one's money. Your retainer letter will give details of how to deal with any concerns. My advice is to discuss those concerns calmly, especially if you think you are paying too much. Everyone makes mistakes and calculating your bill is a human process. It is far more likely that if an error has

been made, it is likely to be human error rather than anything more sinister. If you wish to complain, ask for details of the firm's grievance procedure and arrange to see someone in authority at the firm, to whom you can explain your concerns. You are entitled to ask to see your file, and entitled to request a check of all the items for which you have been charged. Obviously if you have real grounds for complaint, the firm should deal with these. If they won't, or if you wish to report the matter to the Legal Ombudsman, details are at the end of this book. If what you are really after is a reduction of your bill, then say so. If you begin complaining about the case itself and how it was run, in order to gain a reduction, you will put everybody's back up, especially if the outcome of your case has been very favourable.

10. **Be honest with your solicitor at all times.** Don't lie, don't exaggerate and don't waste everybody's time. Lies will be exposed eventually, and could cost a fortune to put right. The most serious cases could also result in a criminal charge of perjury.

Finally: if you are happy with the outcome, please feel free to say so! A *"thank you"* lights up everyone's day.

Breaking the news to your partner

When your spouse learns that you have filed for divorce, they are likely to react in one of a number of ways. They will react with silence, with fury or – most likely – with tears and shock. Remember that the decision you have made has taken time. You cannot expect your spouse to "catch up" and behave as though it were all part of a normal day, if your decision comes out of the blue for them.

People never know how best to tell a partner that a relationship is finished. Some tell their partners in temper; others deliver the news quite calmly. Some ask their lawyers to do it for them, with a lawyer's letter.

Such a letter is bound to cause distress, and I do not enjoy writing to a client's partner. When I am asked to do so I keep the letter courteous, short and simple. Usually I inform the person that the marriage has broken down irretrievably, and that their partner has instructed me to deal with the matter as amicably as possible. I recommend that they appoint their own solicitor as soon as possible.

Breaking the news to your children

How will you tell the children? It won't be easy, but they do need to know. If it is possible, sit down with your partner and tell the children together, having agreed what you will say. Extreme care and sensitivity are required.

Julie Levine, an excellent therapist and counsellor to whom I have referred a number of clients in the past, believes that children are better equipped to cope with divorce if they are involved in the process from the start. She says:

"What earths children is what they know. What they don't know, they fantasise about. Don't try to 'ease them in slowly', because they will feel cheated. Instead, be honest. Tell them that you are getting divorced, and tell them why. If you do not love one another, tell them so. If you have a new partner, tell them this. Make it very clear that nobody is to blame.

How will they react? This is difficult to call, because every child is different. It will also depend upon the strength of the child's relationship with each parent beforehand. If worst comes to worst and the child tries to alienate you, don't give up. Keep talking to them, as they go through the various stages of acceptance."

As a parent, I know that a child who feels safe and secure will thrive. Children involved in marital breakdown will probably have heard their parents argue. They will be scared when their parents quarrel and terrified if they fight. Their parents are their only security. I remember when my father had his 30th birthday. My sister cried at night, because she thought he was so old that he was going to die. At the time everyone laughed and reassured her. But children don't think like adults. They always need to know there is a cocoon around them, and that cocoon is their parents. They need to know also that what's happening around them isn't their fault, and that even though they will soon have two homes, probably new homes, it will be with their parents who love them very much.

With older children, there is sometimes a tendency to treat them as adults and to "lean" on them, letting them bear more of the brunt of the divorce than is good for them. Don't do it, however much they want to play this role. I have seen such situations very often in the course of my work, and noted that as children get older, they long for their stolen childhood. It can scar them. Leave them alone and let them live as children.

I know with my own son that if something was presented to him in a positive way, as something exciting and new, he would accept it. However if he could see worry and fear, it would scare him. How you present the new scenario to your children is vital to their future wellbeing. So make them safe and as much as you can, make it all sound like a happy, thrilling adventure.

11: Taking care of yourself

Learn to manage your emotions

Emotions are very difficult to control during a turbulent relationship breakdown. You may find yourself unable to hide your feelings, and expressing yourself inappropriately. Alternatively you may bottle up your feelings; this, too, can be a mistake. Please don't think that your feelings and experiences are confined to you alone. There are others who are in similar situations and who feel exactly the same as you do.

I keep a regular supply of tissues in my office because it is quite normal for clients to become extremely upset at the beginning of a case. When a client first comes to see me, it is no surprise -indeed, it is almost expected - for the client to break down in tears. Emotions are at their rawest; the pain is at its most intense.

These people can suffer from depression, misery and compulsive behaviour such as drinking or even stealing. Some people will lose weight; others will gain it. Often they may suffer from sleeplessness, rashes, aches and pains, the causes of which are not physical. Coupled with the stress of marital breakdown, these people also have to contend with wholesale gossip about their travails. Small wonder then, that in the initial stages of a divorce, clients can be overwrought and stressed to their limit.

I don't encourage anyone to persist in concentrating on the negative rather than the positive. If something has happened then it has to be faced. The future is more important than the past. The questions of who, why and how are all very well in the short term; in the long term they are harmful. The gossips will soon move on and begin picking over the bones of the next meaty story.

The best remedy is to concentrate on the future. Do your best to leave your problems with your lawyer, who is not emotionally involved and who should always remain professional. Force yourself to do other things and think of other things. Feelings of revenge, bitterness and anger can have no apparent effects on the targets of those emotions. They won't affect your spouse. Some clients can spend a long time feeling sorry for themselves, wallowing in self-pity. But this is not the answer, harsh though it may seem at the time.

The required approach is one of confidence in oneself and in the future, however daunting that future seems. If we were all aware of what was going to happen to us in the future there would not be much point in living, but we do live and tomorrow does come. Given time and a positive, patient attitude, people come through divorce stronger and more self-sufficient than they ever were.

When to seek help

Although my remit is legal, I do consider my clients' well-being to be extremely important. There are depressing studies, which show correlations between divorce and serious illness. An optimistic outlook, meanwhile, has been linked to health benefits including a reduced risk of diabetes and heart disease. One study found a positive correlation between happiness and the fast healing of surface wounds; I believe that this principle holds fast for emotional wounds as well as physical ones.

The majority of clients going through divorce will never become seriously ill as a result. However I do look for trauma in clients and I do my best to ease it.

When you are getting divorced, it can feel as though the world has fallen in. Perhaps life as you know it has ended, has come to a full stop:

- The arguments and the silences are unbearable.
- Money, children, home... The future frightens you. What has happened?
- Everything you are used to and everything you believed to be true has altered and changed. The person you loved and trusted has shattered your trust and destroyed your confidence.
- You have decided to end the marriage because you need an end to the nightmare. There is nothing left between you. You have tried and tried. You have no other choice. Your future cannot be as bad as your present. Can it?
- You are raging inside; you are heartbroken. You cannot clear your mind of all these thoughts.
- Life is spinning round and you no longer feel that you are in control.
- Your future is uncertain, Finances, children, your home... you fear you stand to lose it all.

How do you cope? How do you get through this? Such feelings of distress are normal in the circumstances but are bound to have an effect on you, emotionally and physically.

Most of my clients, when I meet them for the first time, exhibit one or more of the following signs and behaviours.

They are extremely low, or having mood swings. They are experiencing weight gain or loss. They find it difficult to express themselves, speaking in flat monotones and repeating themselves. They may complain of being unable to sleep, of worrying and panicking around the clock. They may be drinking more (never a solution, and never a good idea). They may have difficulty concentrating and giving instructions. Or they may be highly emotional and aggressive because it is all too much.

I am not a doctor but if I note some or all of these signs and I am concerned for a client's wellbeing, I will immediately recommend that they see a doctor or a skilled counsellor. Of course I cannot diagnose depression, but after so many years working in this field, the most important thing to me is to stabilise a client who presents with these problems.

A client who internalises all that stress can become physically ill; furthermore their state of mind may affect the progress of their divorce. On rare occasions our family law firm has represented clients whose instructions have become increasingly irrational and contradictory. They make conflicting demands such as, *"I want you to settle my case NOW!"* together with *"I demand to know the whereabouts of all the hidden money that I am certain exists"*. We cannot do both! Such clients cannot be satisfied, because they are not thinking straight.

Some clients refuse to see a doctor or counsellor. *"I will get through it just fine"*, they say. *"There is nothing wrong with me."* Yet their emotionally charged choices and behaviour suggest the opposite.

In my experience, a client may refuse to seek medical

help because they are scared that if it comes out during their divorce that they are depressed and taking medication (although not every doctor will prescribe medication), the revelations will affect the outcome. They fear that they will suffer financially or worse still, that they will lose their children.

This is simply not true. Please rest assured that you will not be penalised if you have sought help. In fact, your decision demonstrates that you are still in full control of yourself: you recognise that something is temporarily wrong, and you are putting it right.

So if you do feel low and distressed – if you recognise that this is how you are feeling – and you would like to address your situation with the help of a professional, what are you waiting for? Professionals are there to help you. It is their job. Place yourself in their hands. Let them help you. Even if you are prescribed medication it is likely to be a short-term measure that should not affect you adversely and will restore your equilibrium.

Perhaps your GP will be able to spend time talking to you, and that will be all that you need. If it is not, please do consider professional counselling. I have observed that when clients have been to counsellors, the results are often swift and truly amazing. Don't sit there worrying. The restoration of mood, self-confidence and assertiveness works wonders.

When you are able to put your worries into perspective and into proportion, the cold, hard legalities of divorce will become less daunting.

As for quelling your fears about the legal process: that's my job!

The benefits of a solid support network

Feelings of loneliness are commonplace. Relationship breakdown is a terrific leveller, though: it shows you who your loved ones and friends really are.

Family members share in your history, and know a side of you that friends and colleagues do not see. A deep connection can be there, even if you are not especially close to them on a day-to-day basis. Close friends can provide an emotional crutch. If you have been there for them in the past, it is now their turn to provide support and shoulders to cry on. You must be certain that you can rely on their confidentiality. Some friends like to gossip and are not friends at all.

There may be particular times of the day or week that are particularly hard for you: when the house is empty, perhaps, or when you go to the supermarket and weave your trolley around all the couples who are shopping happily together. If you can identify these regular times, you can do something about them: arrange to go shopping with a friend perhaps, or call a relative for a chat.

It is also a good time to expand your social network. Find new people to talk to at the school gate or make new friends at your local "divorced and separated" club. New faces represent new possibilities, and will help you to push away from the past and move towards the future.

Keep on moving!

Physical and emotional wellbeing are essential to a healthy divorce. The Mental Health Foundation stresses the benefits of exercise for mild to moderate depression. I tell all my clients: your body is your temple. Get into shape. Exercise, exercise, exercise!

What do you like doing? Salsa dancing? Going to the gym? Cycling? Running? Swimming? Do anything that will get your heart rate pumping. You will feel better immediately.

I do not advise exercising on your own. It is all too easy to make an excuse and not bother. Instead, find a local group (a running club, perhaps), join a class or get a trainer. That way you have to join in and the habit soon begins to form. If you can't afford it, can you cut back on some other expenses? Of course, if you have a good lawyer, you may be able to get the cost of your workouts added into your maintenance!

One day you think, *"I need a new hair cut"*. Another day you notice that your clothes are better-fitting. Gradually, but certainly within a few months, you will feel and become a different person. Your workouts will have a tremendous effect on your body, mind and spirit.

A new beginning begins with a new you.

Dear Marilyn

Since my partner left, I haven't really had anyone to talk to. My friends are fed up with listening to my problems, my family all live far away and so I spend a lot of time left alone with my thoughts. I have considered seeing the doctor to ask for help, but is it normal to feel like this? To whom can I turn?

Sally

Dear Sally,

You would be abnormal if you didn't feel like this! A partner's departure can be like a bereavement. You are grieving. When people grieve, they go through various stages: shock, denial, anger, grief, bargaining and finally, acceptance. But it can take a long time to reach that final stage.

Support groups may be of help. Virtual support networks such as www.wikivorce.com and www. mumsnet.com are increasingly popular. If you feel that you need it, don't be afraid to seek counselling; see the Useful Resources chapter at the end of this book for contact details. I am a great believer in seeking medical advice. You may need a short course of non-addictive anti-depressants to lift your mood.

Take things as they come: day by day, step by step. You should never try to run before you can walk. Focus on the present and the future, rather than the past. Don't look back. Soon - and it will happen, because time does heal - you will be able to think with more confidence about how you see the New You. Perhaps a new job? A new home? A fresh start? Why not?

Marilyn

Beware of the "faux friends"!

In my experience, friends come in all shapes and sizes and are always loyal, sympathetic and helpful - at least on the surface. However clients often complain that their spouses' friends have encouraged the breakdown of a marriage. They speak with anxiety - and often downright hostility - about the roles played by these people in the lives of their spouses.

A concern of mine is the worrying role that friends can play in divorce. If I hear about one of the following types of "faux friend", or if a "faux friend" appears in my office alongside my client, warning bells will ring.

The thrill seekers: Their lifestyles appear to be incompatible with married life. These faux friends are often newly acquired and may be divorced themselves. They juggle hectic social diaries. For a spouse plodding along in a dull, lifeless marriage, this type of person can possess a magnetic attraction.

"There is so much more out there" such a person might say. *"Ditch him or her, and make the most of your life."* Following nights out together, glamorous lunches and holidays away, even newer "friends" may appear. From a faux friend's perspective, he or she may perceive no wrongdoing. After all, how can it be wrong to sympathise with somebody who has marital problems? How can it be wrong to try and cheer them up? How can it be wrong to help someone have a good time?

The town criers: A faux friend who looks on as a marriage disintegrates may enjoy playing the role of the valued confidante, who is "in" on what is happening. In the worst cases, the more high profile the divorce, the more entertainment and titbit value it offers the faux friends, who egg on the respective spouses. Use your commonsense: you know who the gossipers are, so avoid them.

The know-it-alls: Some friends see themselves as divorce lawyers and counsellors, providing incisive advice. Having been through the process themselves, at first or second hand, they offer plenty of advice about what the client should do, and how the case should be resolved.

These friends are valuable; they provide a good source of support because they have been in your shoes. I recommend that in certain situations, such as when you are choosing your divorce lawyer, you take their advice seriously.

Amongst them, however, there may be certain individuals who see themselves as "divorce experts". These people will dispense continuous commentary and advice as your case proceeds. Yet I have never come across two divorce cases that are identical on facts – and this means that a settlement is never exactly the same. On that basis, it is hard to see how anyone who lacks professional training can possibly give advice. But they do. Worse, they expect that advice to be taken. I can't blame an anxiety-ridden spouse for wanting to follow this advice, but usually it isn't possible because the advice is wrong.

The shadows: These are the faux friends that worry me most. They are seemingly ineffectual and hover in the background during client meetings. Often a client will attend with a trusted "friend" in tow and will insist that this person remains present. The client wants "back up" and likes to discuss the advice I have given after the event. The person will sit through the interview, interjecting with the occasional comment and demonstrating total support if the client becomes distressed.

Call me a cynic, but I'm not overly keen on third parties attending interviews because I don't always trust their motives. How does my client know for sure that the sensitive information shared and careful advice imparted will remain confidential? How does my client know that this chum won't be lunching out on the story in the weeks and months to come? How do we know that it will not end up in the wrong hands? This last one sounds unlikely, but it happens. We have come across cases where the faux friend has turned out to be a real friend –to the other spouse. The faux friend has then imparted details of everything that our client said in the office including, on one occasion, full details of a hitherto unknown affair. That faux friend was also having an affair with the other spouse.

A client should be able to rely upon their legal team 100 per cent. Friends play a completely different role, which is socially centred. It is free of the professional ethics, scruples, obligations, privilege and confidentiality that are the lawyer's domain.

Part III:
Cohabitation &
Civil Partnerships

12: Cohabitation: What You Need to Know

Cohabitation remains a popular choice of relationship in Britain. The number of opposite sex cohabiting couple families has increased significantly, from 1.5 million in 1996 to 2.9 million in 2012. Over the same period, the number of dependent children living in these households has increased from 0.9 million to 1.8 million. I suspect the true numbers are far higher. I worry about the increasing numbers of children who are born to unmarried parents, because there is no body of "cohabitation law".

Unfortunately my office is frequently consulted by an increasing number of cohabitees who have learned, to their great shock, that there is little that the law can do for them following the breakdown of their relationships. Gay couples entering into civil partnerships have the same rights as married couples. However couples who choose not to marry, or who may not be able to marry for a variety of reasons, have few automatic rights in law. In Scotland, there is sound cohabitation law. It does not give couples the same rights as married couples; however it does provide limited redress if the relationship between a cohabiting couple breaks down. I see no reason why such legislation could not be introduced across the rest of the UK. If you read my blog, www.marilyn-stowe.co.uk, which looks at cohabitation law in Scotland in more detail, you will be surprised to discover how favourably it compares to the law in England and Wales.

I was a member of the Advisory Group to the Law Commission, which was asked by Parliament to review this subject and submitted a sensible report in 2007. I have very strong views about what couples' rights are at present, what they should be and what they may be in the future.

If you are cohabiting, you may find that your financial position is precarious if your relationship breaks down. Here is my advice.

What you need to remember

1. Forget about "common law spouses". One survey revealed that 51 per cent of people still believe in "common law marriage", which gives some cohabitees the same rights as married couples. In reality, English law does not recognise such partnerships.

2. If you are a parent, clarify your parental responsibility. The father of a child born after 1 December 2003, if he is not married to the child's mother, has no automatic presumption of paternity unless he has signed the birth certificate acknowledging paternity. *See chapter 24: What's the Deal with Dad?* for further information.

3. Forget about a financial settlement. When a cohabiting relationship breaks down, the financial implications for a non-earner who has little or no money can be very serious indeed. There is no automatic entitlement to maintenance or sharing in the wealth created during the relationship.

DIVORCE & SPLITTING UP

4. There is no property ownership claim unless you can prove your entitlement with hard evidence. The discretion a divorce court has does not exist in cohabitation breakdown. Don't rely on a promise, especially if you make payments or regular contributions towards your shared home. Ensure that you have protected and registered that interest on the property's title deeds, or you may face real trouble if you split. There are various permutations: sole ownership, equal ownership, part ownership, owning a share on a fixed basis or even on a floating basis in proportion to the contribution made by each party. Your solicitor can assist with this. Property ownership should be agreed by a "declaration of trust", registered with the Land Registry. This will help you to avoid expensive litigation in the future.

5. No pension sharing. Pension sharing is available on divorce, but is not available if cohabiting partners split up, or if one partner dies.

6. No tax breaks. Married couples enjoy tax breaks on one party's death or if the couple splits. This does not apply to cohabitation.

CASEBOOK

Ms G came to see me about the breakdown of her cohabitation. She had been living with her partner for 15 years. They had three children together and lived a very good lifestyle. He was a self-made millionaire. Ms G was wearing expensive clothes and told me frankly, albeit incredibly, that she needed at least £5,000 per month just to spend on clothes, shoes, sundries and beauty treatments! She had been very spoiled during the last 15 years, but her partner was clear that he did not want her to work. He thought she should be at home with the children, and that had also suited her.

The problem was her partner. He was a "rough diamond" and sometimes he drank too much. Sometimes he was rude and offhand with her. She wanted to know what she would get if she left him because she felt she had taken enough abuse, especially because she wasn't his wife and felt like a "second class citizen". She wanted to set up home on her own and live her own life - with a huge helping hand.

Ms G was horrifed to learn that despite living with her partner for 15 years, she stood to receive relatively little. Her partner would have to pay for a house for her and the children to live in. The house would be in his name; after the children left school it would pass back to him and she would have to leave. He would have to furnish it and probably buy her a car to ferry the children around. He would have to pay child support for the children and their school fees. He would pay her a "carer's allowance" for looking after the children. But that was it. In short, his duties in law were to his children and none at all to her.

Ms G was shocked to the core. I told her that she would have a much better claim if she married. She started to laugh. Apparently her partner had got wind of her plans to leave, and had proposed to her the week previously!

A few months later Ms G called me. "Thanks for the best advice ever", she said. "I married him. But keep me on your books as I might come back for a divorce."

That was a few years ago and I know they are still together. In this case marriage gave her self-confidence, stabilised both partners and - thankfully - protected their children from trauma.

What to do – while you are together

1. **Put legal safeguards in place.** Just one in six cohabitees who own their homes has a written agreement about his or her share in the ownership. Just one in five has sought advice about his or her legal position. Even fewer couples consider the impact of tax on their wealth. Note also that cohabiting couples can be affected, for better or worse, by rules relating to capital gains tax and inheritance tax.

2. **Enter into a cohabitation agreement.** Unfortunately there is no cohesive law available to cohabitees. Instead these relationships are "regulated" with a hotchpotch of different laws. A cohabitation agreement, also called a "living together agreement", sets out how assets and finances will be divided in the case of a split. Most importantly it will cover where the parties will live if they split up and how this will be paid for. Will

the property be sold or will it remain as a home for one partner and the couple's children? When will an intended sale take place? What about assets, including household contents? A cohabitation agreement can also cover parenting arrangements for children, and the amounts of any payments to a partner and for children. Draft it with the help of a solicitor, so that all the important points are covered. These can include everything from intervals between any payments, to events that could cause the agreement to end. Your solicitor will also draft the agreement in the form of a deed, so that it is legally enforceable.

3. **Women: hold onto your pay cheques and pension!** When a woman pauses her career, her earning potential can diminish. Wives who divorce their husbands are entitled to have their "needs" met, and to share in the couple's assets. Women who cohabit have no such rights. Even if you have no income, no pension and no savings - perhaps because you have devoted your efforts to raising your family - you have no claim. It is inadvisable for a financially dependent cohabitee to give up work or to stop paying into a pension. Even if you stop work, ask your partner to keep making payments into your pension pot. And if you can afford to do so, keep saving for a rainy day.

4. **Make a will.** If you die intestate (without a will) there is no automatic inheritance by your partner, as there is for a spouse. A cohabitee may have a legal dependency claim against your estate, irrespective of a will, if there is insufficient provision made. Other members of your

family, including a former spouse if you still pay maintenance or owe money under the divorce settlement, may also have a claim. When this happens there can be a free-for-all court battle, and legal costs will substantially deplete the estate's value. It is always advisable to take expert advice to avoid such claims. You and your partner should also consider life insurance to protect one another and any children you may have, not least because although married couples enjoy exemption from inheritance tax, cohabiting couples do not and an estate can thus be substantially depleted by the payment of IHT on the first death.

5. **Get your name on the title deeds of your home.** A joint tenancy agreement with a declaration of trust will set out the exact shares owned by each of you in the property, and what will happen if one or both of you wish to sell. . This agreement should be drawn up by your solicitor if you bought your home jointly, or transferred from one of you to both of you if you did not. A written or verbal agreement may also carry some weight, although such agreements are more difficult to enforce.

6. **If the time for such actions has passed** and the relationship has broken down, the following courses of action are available to you.

What to do – after you split up

1. **Tell the taxman (and the benefits office, if appropriate) that you are no longer living together.** Consider your taxation position carefully. Cohabiting

couples are taxed as single people who do not live together. Tax credits are available to lower-income households, and you may qualify. If you are cohabiting and
you own and sell more than one property, you may have
a capital gains tax advantage over married couples. This
is because a married couple is treated as having only
one main residence. However a cohabiting couple with
two residences could qualify for two private residence
exemptions from capital gains tax. On the downside, if
your partner dies, inheritance tax liability could cripple
your finances as no spousal tax exemption is available.

2. **Ensure that children receive financial support.**
   Children are entitled to maintenance, regardless of
   their parents' marital status. See below and "Part VI"
   for further information.

3. **Are you entitled to a carer's allowance?** When a
   cohabiting couple splits up, financial provision for any
   children is covered by an application for child support.
   However if you are the resident parent and your former
   partner is wealthy, he or she will have financial obligations under Schedule 1 Children's Act 1989. If your
   former partner is very wealthy and pays the top rate of
   Child Support, a court can order him or her to pay additional child support called "top up payments". School
   fees, extras and other payments can also be ordered
   against parents, and these can include a car and a lump
   sum. There will be the provision of a furnished home for
   the dependent parent and children until the children
   finish school or college, after which time the provision
   will cease. An income payment to the parent may also

be possible. This is known as a "carer's allowance" and is somewhat akin to spousal maintenance, but again the paying parent must be wealthy and leading a lifestyle sufficient to warrant a comparable lifestyle by the recipient parent. The court has made it clear that it would be unfair for one parent to live grandly while the other does not.

4. **Can the court alter a previous agreement about property?** In certain circumstances, yes. If you do split up and circumstances have changed since you purchased a jointly-owned property or transferred it to joint names, you or your partner may ask a court to make a decision about ownership. For example, if one partner has contributed far more to the property than the other partner, despite an initial agreement that both partners would contribute equally, the out-of-pocket partner can apply to the court to alter the original agreement in his or her favour. Be warned: this is far from straightforward. Complex chancery law applies and you will need expert advice in a field of law that is a minefield.

5. **When the home is in your partner's name, establish that a "trust" has been created.** If a court finds evidence of a "trust", it can rule that the ownership of the property can be shared in some way. If you can convince the court that the property's owner encouraged the belief that you have a share in the property, and you acted on that belief to your detriment, you may be eligible to claim an interest in the property.

6. **Resolve any other property disputes.** If you and your partner cannot resolve your property disputes –

both your home and other items of property – peacefully, you can ask a court to decide. If your partner paid for an item but said that it belonged to both of you, the court may hold him or her to that. Gifts such as jewellery belong to the person to whom they were given. If you owned an item before your relationship began, it remains yours unless you have gifted it or led your partner to believe that they had a share in it. An engagement ringcan be kept by its recipient, unless there was an agreement that it would be returned if the marriage did not take place. Keep an eye on legal fees: don't spend more on lawyers than the value of the property in question, which will be valued by the court at its current or secondhand value, not its insurance or replacement value.

7. **Keep track of credit cards, loans and other financial agreements.** If you borrowed money together, you are both liable for the repayments. Even if one of you takes on the repayments following your split, debt recovery companies can come after both of you if repayments are not met. If this happens, your credit rating could be affected.

8. **Finally...** You may be interested to note that if you cohabit, then marry, the length of the pre-marital cohabitation will be taken into account towards a financial settlement in the event of a subsequent divorce.

Changes ahead

There are calls for changes to the law. Nine out of ten people believe that a cohabiting partner should have a right to financial provision on separation if the relationship has been long-term, includes children and has involved prioritising one partner's career over the other partner's. In Australia the law has changed so that cohabitation breakdown is now treated in the same way as marital breakdown. That's quite a stance and one that I don't think will happen in England and Wales. Too many people, me included, believe that marriage is not equivalent to cohabitation.

When the Law Commission submitted its report to the Government, the report did not equate cohabitation with marriage, but proposed a system of compensation for co-habitees who suffer demonstrable economic loss as a result of the relationship. This approach was sensitive to those who believe that marriage is something more than cohabitation, while countering the substantial injustices that are prevalent at present. The Law Commission suggested a remedy based on any "economic imbalance" that had been the result of the cohabitation, along the lines of the model in Scotland, which has had cohabitation law in place since 2006. The Government of the time announced that it wished to investigate how well cohabitation law was performing in Scotland. Sadly, in 2011 the Government announced that Scottish legislation did not provide *"a sufficient basis for a change in the law"*.

Gow v Grant

Gow v Grant was a Scottish cohabitation case, on which the Supreme Court ruled in 2012. It provides a useful illustration of how cohabitation law can work.

Mrs Gow went to live with Mr Grant in 2002, when she was 64 and he was 58. The couple became engaged. Mr Grant encouraged Mrs Gow to sell her home, which she did in 2003. The proceeds of the sale were used partly for the couple's living expenses. Mr Grant was a college lecturer and Mrs Gow was an audio typist. At Mr Grant's request, when her contract ended in 2003 she did not seek further work.

The relationship ended in 2008. Mrs Gow lived in Mr Grant's home until 2009, when she moved out of his home and into a rented property. By the date the case came to court, the value of Mrs Gow's former property had risen by about £38,000. She had also contributed towards the cost of two timeshares.

Because of the position in which Mrs Gow found herself after she moved out of Mr Grant's house, she brought an action against him in the Sheriff Court in Edinburgh under Section 28 of the Family Law (Scotland) Act 2006. She sought payment of a capital sum, and was awarded £39,500. When this award was overturned by a higher, Mrs Gow appealed to the Supreme Court. The Supreme Court noted the unfairness and and resulting economic imbalance at the end of the relationship between Mr Grant and Mrs Gow, which saw Mr Grant being left with a house and Mrs Gow with nothing, was clear to see. Mrs Gow's award of £39,500 was reinstated.

When the Supreme Court made its judgment, some interesting comments were made about the fairness of the award and the benefits of cohabitation legislation. Lady Hale, one of the Supreme Court's most outspoken justices, said: *"The main lesson from this case, as also from the research so far, is that a remedy such as this is both practicable and fair. It does not impose upon unmarried couples the responsibilities of marriage but redresses the gains and losses flowing from their relationship. As the researchers comment, 'The Act has undoubtedly achieved a lot for Scottish cohabitants and their children'. English and Welsh cohabitants and their children deserve no less."*

Does this mean that cohabitation legislation could yet become a reality in England and Wales? We shall to wait and see. In the meantime, to those who argue that people have a choice whether or not to get married, I say this: there is no point pretending that cohabitation does not exist. It does, and it affects many millions of people here in the UK. Numbers of such families are growing daily. The sooner we have some good laws in place, the better. Not least to protect the children.

13: Civil Partnerships: What You Need to Know

Dear Marilyn

My civil partner and I wish to dissolve our partnership. Must I find a law firm specialising in civil partnership matters, or will any firm do? I mean, dissolution and divorce are pretty much the same thing, aren't they?

Paul

Dear Paul,

You are correct: dissolution and divorce are similar. Every divorce solicitor has a working knowledge of the Civil Partnership Act 2004. So to dissolve your partnership, consult any firm of solicitors specialising in divorce.

Marilyn

The Civil Partnership Act 2004 came into force in England and Wales on 5 December 2005. It gives a same sex couple the right to register their partnership in a ceremony akin to marriage, although the ceremony cannot have any religious connotations and must not take place in religious premises. Civil partners are legally entitled to all the benefits of heterosexual marriage, together with all the tax and inheritance advantages.

If the relationship breaks down, civil partners can apply to the court for the partnership to be "dissolved". They receive the same entitlements as married couples who get divorced. They can apply for financial provision by way of lump sum, property transfer, maintenance and pension sharing orders. Financial provision can also be applied for in respect of any child or children of the family.

A civil partner seeking dissolution is also entitled not to be evicted from the home that the couple has shared and can apply for an injunction order under the Family Law Act 1996 if there has been domestic violence.

The procedure for dissolution of a civil partnership mirrors that of divorce, although different terminology is employed. The equivalent of a petition for divorce is known as an "application for dissolution". A decree nisi is known as a "conditional (dissolution) order".

However you should be aware that one difference between dissolution and divorce is that adultery is not the basis for dissolution. This is because the legal definition of adultery does not apply to same sex couples. In law, adultery is defined as voluntary sexual intercourse between two persons of the opposite sex, of whom one or both are married, but who are not married to one another.

The other four facts sufficient to prove the partnership has irretrievably broken down are:

- Unreasonable behaviour
- Desertion for a period of two years or more.
- Two years' separation, with the partner's consent.
- Five years' separation, without the partner's consent.

Please also note that because the 2004 Act is relatively recent, many civil partners may have lived together for lengthy periods beforehand. If the relationship breaks down, the court may take this period of cohabitation into account when determining the financial settlement.

Prior to the introduction of the Act, same sex couples were more likely to have made financial arrangements such as wills and cohabitation agreements. They may also have operated separate bank accounts. This is good news for the court, because it means that the financial planning between the parties is likely to have been straightforward. Court battles do still rage, however. The most recent, Lawrence v Gallagher (2012) was hard fought but ultimately, the Court of Appeal made its decision as if it had been adjudicating a divorce. Leave to appeal to the Supreme Court was refused.

Part IV: International, Expat and Cross-Border Divorce

14: A Note on Divorce in the UK

In the UK, "English law" applies in England and Wales. Northern Ireland has its own legal system, with law which more or less mirrors English family law, but Scotland stands alone with its own law and legal system. Scotland is an entirely separate jurisdiction, with a very different court structure (except that we share a Supreme Court, based in a superb building in London) and its law is, in many respects, completely different.

We have already seen that Scotland has its own, sensible cohabitation law. In Scotland the divorce process and financial settlements are also dealt with differently. In truth, to those of us accustomed to family law in England and Wales, the differences can be marked. For example, take the case of a non-working wife who is married to a man who was wealthy before their marriage, and who receives a substantial inheritance during their marriage. A divorce in Scotland could leave the wife far worse off, financially, than if the same case was heard in England. In England she could expect to share in all the assets, so that her capital needs and income needs would be met in full. In Scotland, however, she would be entitled to just half the matrimonial assets and a maximum of three years' maintenance. Potentially, she would have no claim upon the assets her husband brought to the marriage, nor upon his inheritance.

In the UK a divorce petition can only proceed in the country in which the parties had their most recent matrimonial home. England and Wales are not split. So if that home was in England or Wales, but the wealthier party relocated to Scotland and then attempted to get divorced there, this could be contested and the Scottish petition would be stayed.

Strict time limits in relation to the divorce petition apply in Scotland, as they do in relation to agreements between the parties. Financial disclosure is necessary before a court can ratify a financial settlement in England or Wales, but it is not necessary in Scotland.

If you are considering divorce in Scotland, or you are currently divorcing in Scotland, you should take advice from a family lawyer there at the earliest opportunity.

15: Expats and the Dangers of a Place in the Sun

CASEBOOK

Mrs E decided to divorce her husband, appointed a solicitor and began subscribing to my blog at www.marilynstowe.co.uk. After reading a post about expat divorce, she had cause for alarm and came to see me. She brought a draft letter, written by her solicitor and intended for Mrs E's husband, who lived in France. When I read the letter, my eyes popped out of my head. It was a letter similar to the letters that we send to spouses in England, informing them of our clients' intentions to divorce.

I was horrified because this letter displayed an ignorance of European law and effectively "tipped off" the husband. Divorce proceedings had not yet been issued and the couple had assets in both France and England. If this letter had been sent to the husband and he had responded by issuing proceedings in France, Mrs E would have been left at a severe disadvantage. For example, the husband had a handsome pension; in England she could claim a share of that pension, but she could not do so under French law.

Mrs E was similarly horrified. She promptly sacked her solicitor and engaged our firm. We immediately issued proceedings in England, protected Mrs E's financial position and successfully secured a number of orders on her behalf.

Around 170,000 couples each year get divorced "across borders" in the EU, and the relevant legislation is increasingly complex. Stowe Family Law's International Law Department receives a steady stream of enquiries from popular ex-pat destinations such as France, Spain, Switzerland and Australia. Some callers wish to know if they can issue divorce proceedings in England. Other clients seek qualified advice about the various legal avenues available to them, drawing upon our firm's expertise in cross-border divorce, asset protection and our network of international legal contacts.

Husbands, who usually stand to lose most from UK divorce law, as it can entitle their spouses to potentially expensive settlements, are increasingly going "forum shopping". They issue proceedings in other countries in a bid to reduce the bill. I am often asked if marrying abroad prevents you from divorcing in England. The answer is no.

In order to proceed in England one or more of the following must apply:

- **One or both parties are habitually resident in England and Wales.** In the case of the Petitioner, he or she must have lived here for at least a year immediately before the petition is filed.
- **Both parties were last habitually resident in England and Wales** and one of them still resides there.
- **The Petitioner is domiciled in England and Wales** and has been residing in England and Wales for at least six months before the petition is filed.
- **Both parties are domiciled in England and Wales.**
- **If none of the above applies and no court in another EU state has jurisdiction,** either of the parties

is domiciled in England and Wales on the date when proceedings begin.

Domicile is a peculiar concept and found only in England. You are born with a "domicile of origin", which you inherit from your father. To obtain a different domicile, you need to sever all your links with your country and put down roots in the new one.

Couples leave the UK for different reasons. Some can afford to give up work and retire. Some move for work. Lower rates of tax are a major draw, especially for the wealthy. In the majority of cases, marriage breakdown occurs after the move, rather than before it.

Unfortunately, in my experience there are sometimes "darker motives" behind a permanent relocation to sunny climes. It is not unknown for husbands to encourage a move abroad as part of a strategy to divorce in the most financially advantageous way possible. On occasion, the hard-heartedness that has gone into the planning and executing of such a plot is scarcely credible. The family moves abroad, the marriage ends - and many wives, when they do not know to whom they can turn, are left stranded. Often they are middle-aged women with teenage children, who have devoted their lives to their families and who are now left shocked and destitute.

Expat cases have their own emotional, legal and financial flashpoints. When marriages and relationships disintegrate overseas, the idyll of a wonderful lifestyle is rudely shattered. Far away from friends and relatives, with no comprehension of local laws and a shaky grasp of the language,and with a desire for things to stay as they are in the face of fast moving change around them, what is to be done?

Typically, I find that a spouse with a game plan consults English divorce lawyers before the family leaves the UK, rather than afterwards. He learns that English divorce law requires a full and frank disclosure of his financial position under oath, and that his wife is entitled to a fair, but potentially expensive settlement. To avoid a hefty claim, he may hotfoot it to the nearest local lawyer in the new country of residence and issue divorce proceedings as soon as the relevant residence criteria have been established.

Eight expat must-dos (especially for dependent wives!)

1. **Take action immediately.** A failing marriage usually includes one party who is in shock, deeply traumatised by what is happening, unwilling and unable to face the future. But that initial period is precisely the one in which they must act decisively. Delays can result in a disastrous outcome. No one facing the devastating loss of a much-loved and trusted spouse wants to pull the plug on the marriage until its end is beyond doubt. But by then, it could be far too late to ensure financial protection.

2. **Contact an English divorce lawyer.** I say this not purely out of self-interest, but because for a person in this situation it is crucial to obtain the best possible advice and stake a legal claim before the partner does. If your marriage disintegrates overseas and you find yourself with someone like me, who is anxious not to let you leave my office without agreeing to issue a petition, take

heart. You can always withdraw that petition later if you wish. But please, protect yourself. Let that opportunity slide and you may regret it. Current EU law states that the divorce will take place in the country in which the proceedings are initiated. For this reason, the first partner off the starting block gains a significant advantage: the luxury of choice. In non-EU countries, the court with the closest connection will deal with the case; but again, not every other country will stay the proceedings and agree that England is the best country for the case.

3. **Issue proceedings straight away, in the most suitable country.** This is a matter for lawyers to advise and is a complex subject because that advice could be challenged in court, especially if there is a lot of money at stake. At Stowe Family Law, for example, we will act in conjunction with a lawyer based in the other relevant country or countries to identify the best option for the client. The English system allows a judge discretion and there must be a fair distribution of assets; in my opinion, this makes our system far more just than its European equivalents, especially for wives who need ongoing spousal support. In European countries, the system of 50:50 capital division of marital assets (as defined by that country) may suit you better. You need to know quickly, because time is of the essence. Another important difference between English law and that of other European countries is the "disclosure burden", which is the legal obligation to disclose financial assets. In other countries, this obligation is frequently much reduced and "shady" assets, which could have been the

reason for the move offshore in the first place, may never surface. If divorce proceedings are initiated in England, all the finances of the parties must be taken into account. In other countries, this is not so. "Non-matrimonial" assets, such as those owned prior to the marriage, may be excluded. Trust assets may also be ignored. If substantial assets are held within the trust, the choice of country could be of critical importance. I once learned about a case in which the capital assets of the parties had been hurriedly placed into a trust by the husband in a second country. Proceedings were then issued in a third country where trusts were not recognised, and never disclosed to the wife. Remember that pensions must also be considered, because there is no point in proceeding in a country if the pension order can never be implemented there. If you are proceeding offshore and there is a pension, check that the mechanism for pension sharing will work before you go ahead.

Experienced divorce lawyers in England and elsewhere should be familiar with cross-border cases, and the complexities that make these divorces so difficult. For additional information, if you are an expat living in the EU, I recommend that you check out a website called www.coupleseurope.eu. It sets out the laws for couples in all 27 EU countries.

Dear Marilyn
My husband and I are both English. We were born in England and we have been sweethearts since

we met aged 14.

We have been married for 26 years. He is the main earner. I don't work. We moved to Spain last year, agreeing to live there for a few years only, before coming back home. We still have a house in England, we have kept our family doctor and dentist, and our children are living in our home. Last month my husband left the Spanish villa we own jointly, taking with him the contents of our shared bank account in Spain. Our English bank account is a long-term deposit account. I think there are other bank accounts in Gibraltar.

Should I file for divorce now, or should I wait and see if we can work things out? Ideally I'd come home and return to our house to be near my elderly parents and our two children, both of whom work in England. My husband has moved to Madrid and is living with a Spanish woman. I'm lonely and desperate. He does pay me some money but I don't think it's enough. I can't get a job because I don't speak the language very well. Is there anything I can do about getting some money out of him in the meantime? Please help - I am desperate.

Tara

Dear Tara,

Stop panicking! Firstly, are you able to apply for a divorce in England? The answer would seem to be yes, because you both appear to be "domiciled" still in this country.

You were both born with a "domicile of origin", which you inherited from your respective fathers. As you have always lived in England, you have never lost your original domiciles of origin. To obtain a different domicile, you need to sever all your links with your country and put down roots in the new one. This doesn't appear to have happened here, so there is no obstacle to issuing a petition straightaway. If your husband has lost his domicile, then you could argue that you are habitually resident and always have been, given you have always had your home in England. At the end of the day, the court must decide which basis applies.

You will need interim maintenance, which we can apply for straight away, and then a further financial settlement. This will include an application for a transfer of property order for the English house, and a lump sum order that may be sufficient to fund a "clean break" for you. Alternatively, there may be a lump sum and continuing maintenance which, after a 26-year marriage, is likely to be for joint lives or until you remarry.

If necessary, legal costs can be obtained by order of the court for a contribution to be paid out of your husband's income, if you cannot obtain any other form of funding - even if he contests jurisdiction and argues the case should be heard in Spain.

Most importantly, we will need to think about asset protection. We need to establish all the assets and stop them being dissipated. In cases where off-shore assets are involved, we may need to consider applying for a worldwide "Mareva" injunction, which will stop your husband from disposing of assets anywhere in the world. We will obtain this injunction in England, and we may need orders in the foreign courts which "mirror" the English injunction, in order to freeze the foreign bank accounts by serving copies on the foreign banks. If you only have a little information, please do not worry too much. In injunction proceedings, your husband will have to file a sworn statement giving details of his entire financial position, and the court will then decide what to do thereafter to protect all the assets until the case is finally resolved. I hope this helps.

Marilyn

Dear Marilyn

I've read all about getting divorced in England. That's all very well but it came too late for me! My husband divorced me very quickly in Dubai and I got next to nothing. I'm back in England now, living with my parents. Is there anything at all I can do? Regards,

Fleur

Dear Fleur,

Don't despair, even if you have divorced overseas! All may not have been lost. It is still possible to obtain a financial settlement in England, even if the parties have been divorced abroad and the recipient spouse has received little or nothing. English law allows unfair settlements to be reconsidered, providing the applicant can demonstrate a viable link with England.

International divorce and finances are examined on my blog, www.marilynstowe.co.uk, where I look at cases and this complicated area of the law in greater detail.

Best wishes,

Marilyn

16: International Divorce and Children

My firm helps people from all over the world who call upon us for assistance. In almost every case, the first questions asked concern the client's children: what can be done to protect them? And what can be done to ensure that contact with the children is not unfairly restricted?

When partners decide to emigrate from the UK, they tend to give little thought to what will happen if the relationship breaks down while they are living in another country. Many parents think that if their children were born in the UK that they will simply be able to return with them from Australia, New Zealand, the USA and so on, but this is simply not the case. Sadly, a lot of parents find this out the hard way.

Browse expat forums, and you will discover many "stuck parents": expats who have been prohibited by foreign courts from moving back to the UK with their children. It is sad to read that so many people feel "trapped" in countries where they do not wish to live. The alternative – returning to the UK and leaving a child or children behind – is unthinkable for most parents. As a result, a parent can be left to grapple with life in a strange country, with no family to support them other than their former partner. The parent is left feeling lonely and isolated, which can in turn have a detrimental effect on the child.

When a court, here or in another jurisdiction, denies an application to leave, this is usually because the court believes that it would not be in the child's best interest to relocate. The child's welfare is of paramount consideration.

Many parents have new wills drafted before they emigrate,

to state what will happen to the children if the parents die while the family is living in another country. Few parents, however, ask a family lawyer to draft an agreement about what should happen to the children in the case of a split. It is advisable to have, at the very least, a discussion about what would happen to your children if your relationship with your partner broke down and one of you wished to return to the UK.

Coming home

If your relationship breaks down and you wish to return to the UK, you need to have the other parent's consent to take the child with you. If you do not have consent, you will need the foreign court's permission.

It can be a lengthy and expensive process to obtain the court's permission, with much emotional turmoil. Some parents spend tens of thousands of pounds in legal fees, fighting to be allowed to take their children back to the UK with them. Having a previous agreement in place could, at the very least, minimise some of this. The parent who wishes to stay could still try and fight it, but the relocating parent could have a stronger case.

The Hague Convention on Child Abduction

Don't be tempted, as so many parents are, to return to the UK and "see what happens". It is understandable why you might want to do this, but it is not advisable. If the country from which your child has been removed is signed up to the Hague Convention, the parent left behind can make an application for the child to be returned. Many of the countries to which Britons emigrate, such as Spain and Australia, are signed up to the Hague Convention.

In these circumstances, if you return to this country with your child, you will be treated as having abducted your child because you have removed them from the country in which they are habitually resident. If a return is ordered, though, it does not necessarily mean that the court has said it is in the child's best interest to live in that country. It means that the foreign country's court has jurisdiction, and that the parent must secure that court's permission to relocate.

Under the Hague Convention, there are certain instances when the court does not need to order that the child be returned. These are as follows:

- If more than one year has passed since the child was removed from the country of habitual residence, and the child is settled in his or her new environment.
- If the other parent consented to the relocation or the court granted permission beforehand or afterwards.
- If *"there is a grave risk that his or her return would expose the child to physical or psychological harm or otherwise place the child in an intolerable situation"*.
- If *"the child objects to being returned and has attained an age and degree of maturity at which it is appropriate to take account of its views"*.

Certain countries are notoriously hard to relocate from. In one case, the court decided that a mother could not relocate from New Zealand to Australia because, due to the length of the litigation, shared parenting had been put in place and appeared to be working. The *"risks associated with parental conflict or the risk that the mother might become isolated to the extent that it affects her ability to be a good parent"* were not sufficient to justify what had become a *"good working solution for the children".*

In the UK, the rules regarding relocation take into account the effect that not allowing the move will have on the parent, and the subsequent effect of that upon the child's wellbeing.

There are many stories of parents being faced with the terrible choice of being stuck in a country where they are unhappy, or returning to the UK without their child. This puts the parent in a terrible position, pitched against a system against which they may feel they cannot win.

Relocating to another country with your child

If a relationship breaks down and there is a child (or children) involved, what rules are applied to cases when one parent wishes to move with the child to another country?

This is called "external relocation" and it is a difficult subject, which can provoke strong opinions. A parent-child relationship can be maintained even when the parent and child do not physically see one another as often as they would like to, but very few parents are going to be happy if their child is moved to another country and the amount of contact is reduced. When one parent wishes to relocate to another country with the children and the other parent opposes that, there is no perfect answer for what should be done.

The test in Payne v Payne

Payne v Payne is an important 2001 case, heard by the Court of Appeal, which sets out the test for the right to remove a child from the jurisdiction. This relocation case and others are examined in detail on my blog by Stowe Family Law solicitor Laura Guillon, but what follows is a summary for readers.

In Payne v Payne, the mother was from New Zealand and the father was from the UK. There was a residence order in favour of the mother and she took her child from the UK back to New Zealand when the relationship broke down. The father brought proceedings under the Hague Convention. The mother had to return to the UK and applied for leave to remove the child permanently. She was successful in her application.

The father appealed this decision, stating that by allowing the mother to relocate to New Zealand with the child, a presumption had been created in favour of that parent. This, he argued, was a breach of the European Convention for the Protection of Human Rights and Fundamental Freedoms 1950 and was also in conflict with the Children Act 1989.

In cases involving children, the child's best interest and welfare are always of paramount consideration and a judge should not make any decision unless it is in the child's best interest. In Payne v Payne, the judge gave some clear guidance as to the considerations for judges when deciding if a parent wishing to relocate with the child should be granted leave to do so. His comments are worth copying here in full:

1. **Pose the question:** is the mother's application genuine in the sense that it is not motivated by some selfish desire to exclude the father from the child's life. Then ask is the mother's application realistic, by which I mean founded on practical proposals both well researched and investigated? If the application fails either of these

tests refusal will inevitably follow.

2. **If however the application passes these tests** then there must be a careful appraisal of the father's opposition: is it motivated by genuine concern for the future of the child's welfare or is it driven by some ulterior motive? What would be the extent of the detriment to him and his future relationship with the child were the application granted? To what extent would that be offset by extension of the child's relationships with the maternal family and homeland?

3. **What would be the impact on the mother,** either as the single parent or as a new wife, of a refusal of her realistic proposal?

4. **The outcome of the second and third appraisals** must then be brought into an overriding review of the child's welfare as the paramount consideration, directed by the statutory checklist insofar as appropriate.

The judge's primary task is always to evaluate and uphold the child's welfare as the paramount consideration – and the inevitable conflict with the adult's rights is secondary. Under the Human Rights Act 1998 a person has a right to family life; when a child relocates to another country with the relocating parent, the non-relocating parent will lose some of that right, but the first consideration is always the child's welfare.

In Payne v Payne, the judge stated that he did not wish to diminish the importance attached to the emotional and psychological wellbeing of the child's primary carer, but that great weight should be given to this consideration when evaluating the child's welfare. He granted permission for the child to move back to New Zealand with her mother.

This decision has attracted criticism. Detractors have described it as outdated, arguing that it does not promote co-parenting because it places too much emphasis on the effect on the primary carer if leave to remove the child is refused.

Shared parenting and external relocation

When a child's care is shared more or less equally, the test is different. Take a case heard by the Court of Appeal in 2011, which concerned a Canadian mother and a Polish father, both of whom lived in the UK. The couple shared the care of their two daughters: the girls spent five nights with their father and nine nights with their mother every fortnight. Although the mother spent more nights with the girls, they spent more daylight hours with their father.

The mother wished to return to Canada following the breakdown of the marriage, as she felt isolated and stressed but on appeal, the father successfully overturned an order permitting the mother to relocate to Canada with their two children. In that case, the judge stated that Payne v Payne was not the correct test to apply when parents share the care of the children equally.

Part V: It's The Money, Honey

17: How It Works

It is not often that both parties to a marriage have the same amount of money. If they had the same amount of income and capital and neither had any debts, then many of the challenges in achieving a suitable financial settlement would be solved.

The usual position is that one spouse has more than the other in terms of both savings and income. Despite the advances of women's rights and careers over the years, some things remain the same. I am afraid that in my experience, it is still usually - but not always - the husband who has more and the wife who has less. Outdated and unfashionable, I know, but in financial terms the husbands are too often the "haves" and the wives are the "have nots". In most cases, the wife is also the one who cares for the children. Added to this mix are overdrafts, tax liabilities and credit card debts.

The court must decide how the net savings and income are to be divided between the two parties. This isn't always easy to do. There is no set arithmetical formula because no couple's case is the same and the law gives the widest discretion to each couple to achieve a tailor-made settlement. If they can't agree what is fair, the court steps in and applies guidelines. It isn't easy, because in many cases, couples cannot live in two homes as comfortably as they did in one home when their income and capital were pooled.

Think about all the families you know and none of them will be the same: they may be young or old, with or without children. These families may be cash-rich or cash-poor. They may have more income than capital. The marriage could be short, medium or long, so needs will differ at different stages of life. One party could have put in far more money in than the other has. One party may be unemployed; the other may have won the National Lottery! One may be disabled or critically ill, and can never work again. In all the thousands of cases I have handled, I have never found one family that is the same as another. There is always something which makes each case different.

For this reason, it isn't easy to divide up all the assets suitably for each family.

The court will deal with all the family assets such as income (net of tax), capital, house (net of mortgage), all capital assets (net of debt) and any pensions. The court may make interim orders for maintenance. It may make longer term orders for maintenance, either for life or a shorter term. It may order payment of a lump sum of capital, transfer property between the parties (including not only land but shares in a company), vary trust arrangements, make a pension sharing order and in exceptional cases, order one party to pay the other's costs.

The overall outcome must be fair and reasonable to both parties. The court must consider first and foremost the welfare of the children, and where the children are to live. It must also consider how soon, if at all possible, the financial obligations of one party to the other can be terminated. Is it possible to have a "clean break", with a lump sum payment? If not, then in order to meet the continuing reasonable needs of the poorer party, the court will make a continuing maintenance order. This can be until considered again by the court or for a fixed term, for life, until remarriage or until the death of the paying party.

If the parties can't agree, what guidelines will the court take into account? When the court reaches its decision the following factors, which can be found at Section 25 of the Matrimonial Causes Act 1973, must be taken into account:

- **Each party's income, earning capacity,** (and any increase in earning capacity either party in the opinion of the court could take steps to obtain;) property and other financial resources. This includes what each party has at the time, and is likely to have in the foreseeable future.
- **Each party's financial needs, obligations and responsibilities.** Again, this includes what each party has at the time, and is likely to have in the foreseeable future. Overleaf you will find an example of one of the most basic budget sheets we use at Stowe Family Law, to help our clients work out exactly what their expenditure requirements are.
- **The standard of living** enjoyed by the family before the breakdown of the marriage.
- **The age of each spouse** and the length of the marriage.
- **Any physical or mental disability** of either party.
- **The contributions made, or which are likely to be made** in the foreseeable future, by each party to the welfare of the family. These include looking after the home or caring for the family.

- **The conduct of each party,** if that conduct is so striking that the court deems it "inequitable" to disregard it.
- **In the case of proceedings for divorce or nullity of marriage,** the value of any benefit which, because of divorce or annulment, that party will lose the chance of acquiring.

The court will divide all the income and capital in accordance with those guidelines.

Visit www.marilynstowe.co.uk to download the Basic Budget Sheets.

stowe
Family Law LLP

EXPENDITURE REQUIREMENTS

Name:

SELF EXPENDITURE	£ Monthly Expenses	£ Annually
Accommodation		
Mortgage		
Water Rates		
Council Tax		
Gas and service contract		
Electricity		
Oil/coal		
Telephone		
Mobile telephone		
Contents insurance		
Buildings insurance		
Repairs		
Maintenance		
Decorating		
Endowments		
Alarm Service		
Cleaner		
Gardener		
Window Cleaner		
Staff		
TV Licence		
Sky TV		
ACCOMMODATION SUB TOTAL		

CASEBOOK

Mr B is 42 and Mrs B is 40. They have been married for 12 years and have now decided to divorce. They have two children, aged 10 and six. Mrs B does not work. Mr B earns £40,000 net. Their house is worth £200,000 after the mortgage is paid off. They have £10,000 in savings and he has a pension worth £40,000. They have credit card debts of £5,000. How will their settlement work?

Firstly, each spouse will each decide where they are going to live and how much that will cost. Mrs B has the children so ideally, she needs a three-bedroom house with a garden. Mr B needs a home too, where the children can come and stay. Mr and Mrs B need to split the (net of debt) capital in such a way that Mrs B - who has reluctantly agreed to work part time - will need a lower mortgage or none at all if possible. Because she receives more of the available capital, Mrs B may agree to receive a lesser percentage of the pension. She will receive maintenance for herself, which will be the amount she needs less her own earned income. She will receive the appropriate level of child support. If she has no mortgage then her maintenance requirements will be less and free up income for Mr B. It is effectively a see-saw exercise to arrive at the right balance for the couple and their children.

So let's set out some home truths about financial arrangements.

1. **Money is a potent weapon.** The person who has it can buy immediate representation rather than waiting for legal aid or other funding arrangements. He or she can cut off the credit cards, refuse to pay the bills and reduce maintenance in order to put pressure on the other side. The person with money can force the other spouse to fight to the bitter end. He or she can afford to take the best advice and use intricate arrangements to disguise finances. At the end of the day, the person with the money is the one who gives and the person without is the recipient. But take heart! I have lost count of the number of clients who say, *"You have never come across anyone like X or Y before"*. When that happens I reply, *"Yes I have. Their twin has just walked out the door!"* I act for people who are similar to one another. I know all the tricks and I know how to deal with them. So take comfort. Unless there is no money there, or far less than you had thought, everything that worries you can be dealt with. Just because somebody lives a flashy lifestyle doesn't mean there is substance behind their style. Be realistic.

2. **Disclosure quickens the pace.** Both parties are obliged to be honest and to reveal full details of their wealth. This is obligatory until a court order is made. The sooner that disclosure is made on both sides, the sooner serious negotiations can take place. However, in practice complete disclosure of a person's financial position is sometimes fudged, the truth is not always made clear and legal costs can be needlessly incurred in trying to sort out exactly what income and assets are being

dealt with. The pursuit of assets can incur extremely high costs, especially when estate agents, accountants, actuaries and pension specialists begin sending bills. And don't forget the barristers, some of whose charge-out rates are breathtaking.

3. **A financial settlement can be tailored to a couple's needs.** It does not have to follow a set pattern. All sorts of permutations can be used in order to achieve a satisfactory settlement. Payments of capital (known as lump sum payments), can be paid in instalments. An agreement can be reached about the division of a pension, redundancy pay, or property to be sold in the future. Settlements can be flexible. Just because one couple's case has been settled in a certain way, doesn't mean that your case will be settled that way too.

4. **Trust, company, and pension law is a minefield and tactics need to be considered from the outset.** If your case involves complex assets, make sure your solicitor is aware of this as soon as possible and understands fully how each of these assets would be dealt with in a divorce. If a suitable approach is left too late, your divorce case could be irreparably compromised. You must remember that trusts, companies and pensions are all separate bodies. The assets are not automatically yours or your spouse's, unless ownership is demonstrated by the accounts. It is difficult to value and divide such assets and there can be tax consequences. For these reasons, such work should be undertaken by a specialist. We will look at this in more detail later.

5. The following statements are myths:

• That the house and assets will always be split 50:50. The starting point for division of surplus assets will be 50:50, after the parties' needs are met. A departure from this may mean that the court is taking into account assets acquired before the marriage, inheritances and gifts and even a "stellar" contribution by one party to the assets, which is so spectacular that it would be wrong to divide the assets equally.

• That the wife will not be entitled to maintenance if she works. Maintenance is assessed on reasonable "need".

• That the wife will not be entitled to maintenance if the children are above a certain age. Again, maintenance is assessed on reasonable "need".

• That the wife will not be entitled to maintenance at all if she also receives a capital settlement. The law does not work that way. The words "fair" and "reasonable" are key to any settlement, to meet both parties' needs in terms of both income and capital.

• That the wife will not be entitled to share in capital after all her needs are met. Only the richest people on earth need worry about these "stellar contributions", but I mention them here, just in case you are one...

CASEBOOK

Mr F and his wife were in their early forties and had four children. Mr F earned £80,000 a year net of tax; his wife earned £15,000 a year net of tax.

They had a life policy with a surrender value of £12,000. Their house was worth £450,000, with a mortgage of £50,000. His pension was worth £50,000; hers, £30,000.

Selling the family home would have raised £200,000 for each of them. This would have been ample for Mr F to start again, but £200,000 would not have been enough for his wife and children to make a fresh beginning in a new home. Mr F's salary was not high enough to support him in a new home, while paying child and spousal maintenance.

This was a relatively amicable split, and I was able to propose a number of realistic solutions that potentially suited all parties. We ultimately agreed that Mr F would pay maintenance for his wife of £20,000 per annum, to help her with her outgoings with no cut-off date, and he would also pay child support for the children until they finished school, To secure the maintenance in the event of his death, he would pay the premiums on a policy of life insurance. Mrs F would also accept two thirds of the equity in the house. They kept their own pensions and split the insurance policy equally.

The other options were as follows:

In exchange for all Mr F's interest in the house, Mrs F could have relinquished her entitlement to maintenance. They could have split the pension and he could have got more capital out of the house.

Or Mrs F could have agreed that at some point

> *in the future, Mr F would receive a share of the house. In the meantime he would have paid main-tenance, kept his pension and kept all the insurance policy. When he did get his share - perhaps when the children left full-time education, whether sec-ondary or tertiary, or if Mrs F remarried or perma-nently cohabited - Mr F would have probably had to pay capital gains tax on his share. Furthermore this arrangement would have put pressure on Mrs F to raise an inflated lump sum to keep the prop-erty. However this arrangement would have been a means to keep her and the children in the house.*

Maintenance can be open-ended or for a fixed term, which means it finishes at the end of that term or may be reviewed on the occurrence of a certain event or date in the future, or by an application to the court for the order to be varied or termi-nated. Maintenance payments to a spouse end automatically on remarriage or death. Maintenance is a very valuable asset and that entitlement should never be given up lightly. Equal-ly, if you are liable to pay maintenance on an open-ended ba-sis and you can negotiate a clean break, then try and do so!

Maintenance does have a "sting in the tail": a potential li-ability to capitalisation (payment of a lump sum) if the payee has the ability to do so in the future. Capitalisation is usual-ly based on a lifetime award of maintenance or can be for a lesser term, depending on the circumstances. It can also be assessed on what the payee should have been paying if his or her income has increased in the meantime. The calculation is carried out by reference to what we call the Duxbury Tables.

CASEBOOK

Mrs S was 52 and had two grown up children. Mr S was 53 and earned £300,000 net per annum. Their house was worth £5 million with no mortgage. Mr S had a pension fund of £1.5 million.

Mrs S required £1.5 million for her housing and had a budget of £100,000 per annum for her income requirements. She received an equal division of the equity in house (£2.5 million) and a clean break that took her surplus £1 million of capital into account. She would receive sufficient income, supplemented by a payment from her husband's share of the house and his pension fund, to give her £100,000 a year for life.

This calculation was made by reference to the Duxbury Tables. The computation first arose in the case of Duxbury v Duxbury. The tables give a capital figure, assuming a net of tax income need for either a man or woman for life. The calculation assumes a relatively low rate of investment return, and that some capital will be spent so that on a part investment return, part capital spent basis, the sum provided will be spent at the end of the person's life, which is actuarially calculated.

This is not the same as an annuity, which is much more expensive to provide. The Duxbury Tables do take into account an uplift for inflation.

More specialist Duxbury programmes, such as the amount of capital required to provide a specific income up to or from a certain age, can factor in other capital income and pensions.

If you are about to receive a clean break in exchange for relinquishing your maintenance, you should ask your solicitor to check what you are receiving against the Duxbury Tables, to ensure that you will be properly provided for - and for many people, that means for life.

If you are representing yourself, you can access the Duxbury Tables by subscribing to At a Glance, a family lawyer's "bible" published by the Family Law Bar Association. At the time of writing, At a Glance costs £50 and can be purchased from www.classlegal.com. Please note, however, that the contents of this book include lots of figures and tables, which may be daunting for the uninitiated. If in doubt, ask a lawyer for help.

Not every spouse will be in such a fortunate position. However if your spouse is earning a substantial income, if there is plenty of capital and if you are entitled to lifetime maintenance, I would be hesitant to advise a clean break unless it can be paid out in full. A bird in the hand is worth two in the bush, but what seems a vast amount at the time may not seem so sizeable ten years later!

What happens to the house?

When you decide that enough is enough and divorce is the only way out, your main priority is the welfare of your children. Accommodation is likely to run a close second.

Disposal of the family home can be one of the most traumatic aspects of the whole divorce process. You have lived there for years and it holds memories of happier times, yet you are being forced to sell it because your partner has fallen for someone else. It hardly seems fair, does it? This is the position that thousands of people find themselves in every year.

What can you do, while you are waiting for your divorce to come through?

- **Be practical.** First and foremost, force yourself to consider the situation as objectively as you can, even under these difficult circumstances.
- **Stay awhile.** If your husband or wife has found someone else, the chances are that he or she will want to move out to be with the new partner. But if the cause of your divorce is less clear cut, the longer you can both stay together the better you will be able to plan for, and afford, life apart. It may not be in your interests to leave, and a way may be open for you to stay. So don't rush to put up the for sale sign. But don't be bloody-minded either. If it is clear the house must be sold, don't delay, although you shouldn't move out until you have somewhere to go - preferably your next permanent home. If one of you leaves before the divorce is finalised, you will have to maintain two properties on an income which previously maintained one. Even if the plan is to buy two smaller houses, do make sure the family home is sold before you plunge into the property market. Otherwise you could be caught out and burdened with indefinite bridging loan

repayments. Each case needs to be considered on its own facts, but I have come across many wives in a hurry to settle, who agreed to a sale - and then had cause to regret it later on, when it became clear they could have stayed or obtained more than 50 per cent of the proceeds.

- **Work out who will pay for what.** If staying under the same roof really is out of the question, make interim financial arrangements. If your partner is the breadwinner, can afford to maintain two homes for the time being and is willing to do so, then fair enough: this plan may suit both of you. But don't rush into that decision. Relinquishing hold of what is a major asset means that if your spouse wishes to delay the sale, it will be much easier if you aren't physically there. One of my clients somehow managed to delay the sale of his home for five years after the court ordered a sale. His wife bitterly regretted her decision to move out.

- **Stay behind the wheel.** If your partner moves out and promises to keep up with the mortgage and all the out-goings, don't put yourself in the position of finding you are months in arrears when payment hasn't been made. Make sure you know for sure, every month, that the mortgage and other bills have been paid, either by getting the money from your spouse direct, or by checking that it has all been paid. Some building societies estimate that up to 40 per cent of their arrears are due to divorce or separation, so they understand the problem and will do their best to help. Next, contact your solicitor and ask for an interim order to be obtained to make your partner pay. If your partner's name is on the mortgage, it will clearly be in their best interests to do so. If the house is eventually repossessed, your partner will lose money too and will find it very difficult to obtain another mortgage in the future. If your partner still refuses to pay and you take over the payments, you can argue that you are entitled to a larger share of the property when it is eventually sold. Approach your bank manager for an overdraft. The court cannot ignore the existence of a loan when making the final orders on your divorce. This may be more practical and cheaper than going to court for an interim order. Make sure your solicitor notifies your spouse that you are doing this, and give your spouse the opportunity beforehand of clearing the arrears by stating that you will be claiming not only the amount of the borrowing at the final hearing but also interest and the costs of so doing. If you need to, contact the Benefits Agency for help. They may well be able to assist you.

These points deal with some of the practical arrangements prior to divorce, but what of everyone's needs afterwards? Here's a home truth: unless you have substantial liquid assets available, selling the family home is often the only way that a couple can afford two properties. Fortunately, ways around this can sometimes be found.

Note that if you separate from your spouse for some years, with just one of you continuing to put money into the property, the time and money put into the property during the intervening years will certainly be taken into account. This could mean that the partner who made the investment could be able to extend their mortgage by a sufficient amount to buy out the other partner's reduced share.

Every case centres upon the specific income and capital of those involved and their needs. As unfair as it may seem at the time, the courts are simply not interested in bad behaviour and who left whom. Guilt doesn't come into it: even if your spouse deserted you, he or she still retains the rights to a share of the assets. If it comes to it, and taking both parties needs into account, a court can order you to sell and make that order in the interests of "fairness". You may not think fairness should work that way, but the courts have made it clear that irrespective of the moral rights and wrongs - which can be interpreted in many different ways - the practicalities are what concern them, especially in relation to the children.

If the prospect of a move seems unbearable right now, and I do fully understand that it may be, I would suggest you think of it this way: a happy, small home is infinitely better than an unhappy, large home. If it means being able to put a bitter relationship behind you and starting life again, mortgage-free, moving house is a small price to pay.

Pension planning

Dear Marilyn

My husband and I are divorcing after eighteen years of marriage. I have heard from my husband that I may not claim against his pension, but as I am approaching retirement age I'm very worried, because I have very little pension of my own. What can I do?

Margaret

Dear Margaret,

Male clients are often displeased to discover that financial negotiations extend to their pensions. They are also shocked to discover that, if the wife is younger than the husband, her claim to a share of the pension can potentially be greater than his because her life expectancy may be greater than his.

Do ensure that the pension scheme is properly valued by someone properly qualified to do so. Your lawyers will know of specialists in the field. If you are acting on your own, search out a fully qualified pension specialist who has experience of divorce and pension sharing. The reason for caution is also because not every pension is accurately valued by the pension holder, as there are different ways of valuing pensions. If the pension is held in property, you will need to consider when that property was last valued, and do not rely on the accounts. I think the largest discrepancy we have ever uncovered at Stowe Family Law was a pension that seemed to be worth about £400,000 and was in fact worth more than £1 million. So please, don't rely on a simple piece of paper! Get it checked.

Would you be better off with capital or with a pension fund? It may be that if your husband is determined to hold onto his full pension, there are other assets he can offer that can be offset against your share. An enhanced share in the family home, *for example. You need to consider the pros and cons with your solicitor, although a future inflation-proofed income is well worth having.*

Marilyn

It used to be said that an Englishman's home was his castle. These days it is likely to be his pension that he guards most jealously, especially when divorce raises the prospect of sharing the proceeds with his former wife. Negotiations over allocation of pension funds can be the most acrimonious and bitter of the entire divorce. In many cases, after the family home the pension is the largest financial asset involved in a settlement.

If the husband is the breadwinner, he may well regard the pension as his reward for a lifetime of work. This is particularly evident in those jobs and careers that demand long and unsociable hours, do not pay excessive salaries but offer generous pension provision at the end.

In such cases the husband will often choose to disregard the fact that it was only the support of his wife that enabled him to work so hard. Caring for their home and children was really her "contribution" to creating the financial safeguard for their life after retirement. The wife will certainly believe that she is entitled to an equal share.

Following legislation that came into effect in 2000, pensions may now be divided whatever the nature of the pension, and whether or not it is already being paid.

- **Your lawyer's task is to establish the pensions that are in existence.** They will, with professional advice, value the schemes to establish the Cash Equivalent Transfer Value. This is not always as straightforward as it could be, so it is vital to obtain advice. Projected future benefits must also be considered. Your lawyer will note the terms of the pension: any lump sums on retirement, regular income, death in service benefits, death benefits after retirement, transfer to other schemes and widows benefits. Once a value is obtained (sometimes this requires negotiation between the valuers, or obtaining values of assets that are in a pension fund), the value can then be divided between the parties. A transfer takes place to a new pension, established for the benefit of the person who seeks a pension share. Again, professional input from specialists is invaluable to make sure the new pension value is maximised and continues to be a realistic asset.

- **A note of caution:** your lawyer should, of course, ensure that all pension schemes are disclosed during negotiations. Other non-contributory pension schemes run by employers, Additional Voluntary Contributions made by a spouse and SERPS payments can sometimes slip through the net. Entire schemes have been known to go undiscovered, placing the non-breadwinner in a losing position.

The courts use their discretion when making settlements. A 30-something wife is unlikely to end up with much, if any, of her husband's pension. A 50-something wife, whose husband has a large pension pot, can expect a good share even if the marriage has been relatively short, depending on her needs. If the court can award a clean break settlement, it will.

A note on applications for a financial remedy

We have considered how the court might divide up assets, but what is the procedure? I tend to issue an application to the court, using Form A, as soon as divorce proceedings are underway. I have previously mentioned that I don't like to wait because it can cause delay and add to the costs. Rather, I like to get things sorted as soon as possible. Many people are being headed off to mediation, but in most cases I think this is useful only when full disclosure has been obtained, and is sufficient to rely upon. So along with the petition, I normally issue Form A. This is the application for a full financial settlement, known as an application for a financial remedy. You can download Form A from the link to court forms at www.justice. gov.uk. There will be a court fee to pay but in some cases, this can be waived or reduced. The court clerk will assist you.

At the time of writing, there are moves to oblige all couples to attend a mediation information meeting beforehand. Even if this becomes reality, it is hard to see what will be achieved in cases where disclosure is required - except lengthen the case, add to the costs and, when couples do proceed with mediation straightaway, result in potential injustice for the weaker party.

First Appointment

After an application for a financial settlement has been issued by the Court, a date will be set for the First Appointment, which takes place after both parties have completed their Form E. This is a lengthy document, designed to give full and frank disclosure of their financial positions and future requirements. There will usually be a number of questions arising following exchange of Forms E, which takes place 35 days later. There will be other information to obtain, such as valuations of assets if the parties cannot agree what the assets are worth. However the court decides what questions and valuations are required. In practice many parties do agree but in more complicated cases, when both sides want pages of questions answered and a host of valuations, the court is the final arbiter.

Before the hearing the parties must exchange draft questionnaires. These contain queries about the other party's Form E. Each party will also file a chronology with relevant events and dates, and a statement of issues setting out what they believe to be the relevant matters for the court to consider. These documents should give the judge an idea of where each party is coming from. A schedule of costs for both sides, giving details of legal fees to date, will also be taken into account by the judge.

The First Appointment is usually a fairly short hearing, which takes place in a private room rather than a traditional courtroom. Usually the judge sits at the head of a table, dressed in everyday clothes. The lawyers and clients sit either side. The parties, unless representing themselves, do not speak.

The judge will consider what, if any, additional information is required before meaningful negotiations to settle can take place. The parties do need to attend this hearing and if they wish to be excused, will need permission of the judge. It makes sense for them to be present, to ensure that nothing is left out and that they understand how the case is going to proceed.

Both sides will put their positions to the judge and explain what, in their opinion, is still deficient and needs to be produced. Valuations of assets, when there is a dispute about value, may be ordered, often with a single expert jointly appointed by the parties at joint cost. Sometimes the judge may allow each party to have their own expert, but it depends on the type of asset, the value in dispute and the complexity and cost of the valuation involved. Further disclosure may be ordered of the parties themselves if the disclosure to date is unclear or incomplete. The judge will fix a timetable for all the events to happen and for the next hearing: the Financial Dispute Resolution Appointment.

The process has begun in earnest.

During the period between these two hearings, a lot of work needs to be done. For example, there must be valuations, answers to questionnaires, consideration of answers, tax advice, consideration of omissions, perhaps additional court orders, examination of assets, and consideration given to how assets can be divided. The documentation must be shipshape. The court will also be told how much has been incurred in legal costs to date.

Financial Dispute Resolution

A Financial Dispute Resolution hearing (FDR) is a court appointment that takes place "off the record", during which a divorcing couple can be helped by the judge towards a financial settlement.

A typical FDR proceeds in a small room, for all but the most complicated cases, where lack of space requires a larger, more traditional courtroom. After an application has been issued to the court and formalities such as financial disclosure and valuations have been complied with, both parties will usually file with the court a skeleton argument about their respective positions, and (again) a schedule of costs, which sets out the costs incurred to date. They will also file offers made to settle. At this stage, the intention is that the parties are given the opportunity to settle the case at a hearing that will take place entirely "without prejudice", similar to mediation.

A judge hears the parties' lawyers - or hears the parties themselves, if they are unrepresented - and attempts to bring about a settlement. The parties are not called upon to give evidence, but listen to the arguments advanced on their behalf. The judge will have read the details of the parties' respective positions beforehand. (Tip: make sure you read and approve the skeleton argument before the judge sees it. Often it may be prepared by your barrister the day before the case, so make sure you ask to see it before it is lodged with the court and check that you agree with what it says). The judge indicates how the case is likely to play out, and the parties then go away to try and reach an agreement between themselves.

The problem I have occasionally encountered with an FDR is when the judge doesn't handle the procedure too well. I've seen quite a few cases where I think the judge has tried to be so impartial that he or she has simply thrown away the opportunity to settle the case. By being too impartial, the judge gives false hope to the more aggressive party and can bring despair to the weaker party.

I recall one case in which a judge wasted an entire afternoon in Central London, in discussion with a barrister about the latest case law. Neither client was impressed and the case came nowhere near a settlement, although we all heard a lecture about family law and financial settlements from the judge.

Sometimes judges can be far too weak and can be bullied by an overly aggressive lawyer. In trying too hard to reach settlement, the judge can make suggestions that benefit neither party. All parties leave court regretting the waste of time and worse, the waste of costs, bemoaning a less than perfect legal system that relies on the approach of just one person - and which can then cost the parties thousands.

This may suit a more aggressive spouse who has made the decision that, as there are only the costs of the final hearing left to pay, it might be worth taking the gamble and continuing on to the final hearing. Since each party only pays their own costs, and is not at risk of paying the whole of the other side's costs, this tactic has become more widely used.

A successful outcome means that a couple can walk away from court ready to begin new lives. An order can be drafted on the spot if it is fairly straightforward. Otherwise, an agreement reciting the heads of terms reached will do for the time being, as long as it is signed. If both parties sign up to the agreement, it is very difficult to backtrack if somebody changes their mind at a later date.

An unsuccessful outcome means that the case continues. When this happens legal costs will mount and several months later, a battle will be fought out in court. As I hope I make clear, the cost, stress and worry of such a battle should never be underestimated.

On the other hand, if you are being bullied by someone who will only settle on poor terms and you have good advice that you can do better, take that advice and stand firm! The final hearing is not as bad as you might think. All the documents and offers lodged by both parties will be returned to the parties as if they had never existed.

The final hearing could be months away. In London it might be in nine months' time. It may still be possible to settle in the meantime, so don't give up. But if one party thinks the other is being ridiculous (usually both sides do) or if there is a lot at stake, either money or principles, then a hearing will take place. If this happens, make sure the interim financial arrangements are all agreed as part of the directions necessary for the case to go to trial. Remember to include orders for updating the statements of both parties and valuations.

Again, a good deal of preparation is required to ensure the judge has a full set of papers for the final hearing. This preparation includes pleadings, correspondence, up-to-date valuations, up-to-date financial disclosure from both sides with skeleton arguments, details of open offers made (not confidential offers made without prejudice) and a schedule of the costs incurred to date. This judge will not have conducted the FDR and will not know of any offers made at the FDR.

Court Hearing

If all else fails you will have to attend this final hearing. (Final, that is, unless you appeal.)

Again, as with the previous hearings, it is unlikely the hearing will take place in a traditional court room. The judge moves out of his chambers only when the case is complex and additional room is needed for all the lawyers, experts and bundles of documents. For most people, there are no imposing court surroundings to worry about. There is no dock. You will sit with your solicitor and barrister.

I suggest that at all times, you treat this hearing as coolly and as commercially as possible. If you are nervous, remember that nerves are natural. The day will pass, the hearing will soon be over and life will continue.

At this hearing how you behave and in particular, how you answer questions will count. Until now your lawyers have done all the work and you have sat back and listened. This time, you too will have to add your bit.

Ask your solicitor how to dress, how to conduct yourself and how to address the court. Read chapter 28 of this book, "How To Act In Court", for further information.

When preparing for your hearing, remember to read your Form E beforehand so that you know exactly what has been said and what you are claiming. Read your spouse's Form E too. Ask to read all the other relevant documents, including the skeleton arguments of both sides for the Final Hearing, which will differ from those lodged for the FDR. Make sure you understand them. Above all, make sure the information given to the court by both sides is current and correct - not months out of date, dating back to when the case first began. Remember: valuations can go up and down. Redemption figures for a mortgage may have altered. Pension values may have altered. Share valuations may have altered. Debt amounts may have altered. Revalued assets can have a big effect upon a settlement.

If you don't understand or are uncertain about anything,

ask your lawyers and remind them. Make notes. If you remain proactive, you will keep them on the ball and may also keep your costs down. Lawyers argue on the law and facts as they understand them, but they cannot be expected to have your relatively detailed knowledge about events or circumstances. So if the assets are inaccurate, or if the facts are inaccurate or misrepresented, make sure you are in a position to refute them.

If offers are made at the door of the court, consider them. If it is still possible to settle, don't dismiss offers out of hand. Some lawyers like to battle, come what may - but if you want to settle, say so.

18: Order, Order!

For many people a financial order, or settlement, represents the final chapter in a divorce. Generally, it comes as a huge relief to all concerned. Parties can begin to rebuild their lives, putting the unpleasantness of a break-up behind them. For those who secure a "clean break" settlement, it will most likely be the end. For those who continue to pay or receive maintenance, however, this is not necessarily the case.

Facts about financial settlements:

- **The court will want to know what is to happen to the children,** where they will live and with whom they will live. This will help the court to determine the size and type of housing required.
- **The length of a marriage will affect the size of a settlement,** depending on when the assets of the marriage were accumulated. In law, a "short" marriage is reckoned to be up to five years. A "medium" marriage is between six and 14 years' duration. Thereafter a marriage is regarded as a "long" one.
- In recent years, high profile cases have resulted in large payouts to wives, because the courts must now apply the principle of "sharing" the financial fruits of the marriage between the parties.

The court will want to see the budgets for both spouses and the children, in terms of future income and capital needs, all of which will be set out in your Form E. It makes no sense to exaggerate or underplay your budgets. The judge won't be impressed or swayed. Your future housing need and income requirements are some of the most critical parts of your Form E, so investigate and do your homework before submitting this information to the court.

Your solicitors will give you budgetary advice, but if not, the "Form E Budget Worksheet" featured overleaf will be a useful starting point. If you have more than one child, vehicle or property, a separate budget can be prepared for each if necessary. This means that the separate costs can be identified far more easily, and shown on the summary as such. A printable copy of the Form E budget worksheet can be downloaded at www.marilynstowe.co.uk.

Visit www.marilynstowe.co.uk to download the FORM E Budget Worksheet

stowe

Family Law LLP

HOUSING SCHEDULE 1

	Current (£)	Estimated future (£)
Property 1 (insert address)		
Mortgage		
Endowment policy		
Water Rates		
Council Tax		
Gas and service contract		
Electricity		
Oil /coal / other		
Telephone		
Contents insurance		
Buildings insurance		
Repairs & maintenance		
Replacement & servicing of electrical appliances		
Decorating		
Alarm Service		
Cleaner / domestic help		
Gardener		
Handyman		
Window Cleaner		
Staff		
Cleaning materials		
Pest control		
TV Licence		
Sky TV		
Boiler / central heating maintenance		
Linen / bedding		
Total costs per month		

- **The court will examine each spouse's future earning capacity** and, if applicable, set this against their maintenance needs both before and after retirement. For example, can you go out to work if you haven't worked for the last 10 years? If so, what will your position be and how much will you earn? What could you reasonably do? Will you need retraining? Can you work if there are young children to look after?

- **I recall one client in her 50s, whose husband earned £450,000 per annum.** There is no point arguing, as this man did, that his spouse should take a job as a checkout assistant at a supermarket. The judge took the view that she should not work at all. On the other hand a judge might require a mother with children to work, at least part-time until the children are older. Much depends on the judge and the facts of the case, but it makes sense to contribute towards your cost of living.

- **The court will take new relationships into account.** For example, if you are living with a new partner in your new partner's home, the court may deem your financial needs to be reduced or extinguished altogether. After all, some or all of your maintenance needs are being met. Remarriage will always end a claim for maintenance - but not for capital, if this has not been fully resolved beforehand.

- **The question of how much must be paid in each case is often a tough one to answer.** This is because an analysis is required not only to ascertain the family's net worth, but also to assess how and when that worth was acquired. If it is determined that the assets are "matrimonial", they should be shared between the parties; if they are "non-matrimonial", they could be excluded. In the majority of cases this point is irrelevant, because there is barely enough to meet the parties' needs. It applies when there is a surplus of assets over needs. Once needs have been met, how will that surplus be divided? Increasingly the view is that non-matrimonial assets should be ring-fenced once reasonable needs have been met. What is "reasonable", however, may vary from one case to another, depending on the parties' standard of living during the marriage.

- **Spousal maintenance may be paid for a period of time**, with the court reserving the power to extend that period - or not, as the case may be. Maintenance may cease on cohabitation and will automatically end if the recipient remarries.
- **In other cases, maintenance will have no cut-off date** and will only cease on the orders of the court, or on the death of one of the parties.
- **If one of the parties wishes to bring an open-ended maintenance order to an end,** this may occur by mutual consent. Both parties may agree upon the payment of a lump sum in lieu of future maintenance. Or they may agree that the time has come for the order to cease, the recipient spouse being able to manage alone. Solicitors are consulted usually when there is no such agreement, and one party does not want to end or reduce the obligation.

Please note that maintenance for children is covered in greater detail in chapter 23.

Changing a maintenance order

This is called a "variation of maintenance order". The costs will be high, and a result obtained for either party is likely to be disproportionately expensive. There aren't any winners. I don't recommend this unless it is absolutely necessary and legal costs are not an issue. In most cases the relevant court will be the court where the order was made.

The best way to avoid such an order is to include an automatic increase within the original agreement. It could rise in accordance with the retail prices index. Or it could take the form of a percentage increase in line with the payer's income.

In a straightforward case, it makes sense to negotiate or proceed via the Magistrates Court. This is a simpler and cheaper process, which involves registering the order in the Magistrates Court. Note that when larger sums of money are involved, an experienced judge should make the determination.

A "clean break" settlement or continuing maintenance

The law states that the financial obligations between spouses should be ended as soon as possible after the end of the marriage. Maintenance, however, is paid to the former spouse post-divorce because he or she requires it. The amount will be agreed between the two of you, or by a court if agreement is not possible. Sometimes, when there is enough capital to cover future maintenance needs going forward, a "clean break" can be achieved. If you end up paying continuing maintenance, it may be that you prefer to do so rather than a lump sum - although if a court makes the order, it will usually go for the "clean break" option because of the law.

You may reason that your former spouse is likely to remarry, whereupon maintenance will cease. This makes maintenance a more cost-effective option.

However, as I've mentioned earlier, if you can afford a "clean break" settlement at the time of your divorce, this can be the best course to follow. It is an order for a one-off payment, which relieves both parties of any future financial obligations to the other. In essence, it means that there will be no "comebacks" in the future.

If you are in receipt of maintenance you can apply for a lump sum of capital at a later date, in place of the continuing payments. This is called "capitalisation of maintenance".

It may have been that a clean break was impossible at the time of the divorce, due to insufficient capital. Years later, the financial positions of both parties have altered. Your partner may have rebuilt their capital and be about to retire. If their overall income is about to reduce, they may wish to pay you off so that they can hold onto all of their pension. If you are living with a partner, this can make for a bitter battle. Why should maintenance continue to be paid?

Dear Marilyn

In my consent order, a clause was included whereby my ex-wife's lifetime periodical payments would cease if she began cohabiting with a new partner. At the time of the hearing, I was fully aware that she was already in a serious relationship. She has remained in that relationship. Her partner has now sold his house 20 miles away and has purchased a new property less than 200 yards from my ex-wife's house – our former family home, which I was ordered to donate to her.

It is clear, isn't it? They are "living apart together" in order to thwart the term "cohabitation" in the consent order. So I have decided to apply for cessation of periodical payments, on the grounds that she is in a firm and committed relationship that is a quasi-marriage, in two separate houses, in order to keep the periodical payments alive.

What are my chances?

Rob

Dear Rob,

Maintenance payments are based upon "reasonable need". Determining reasonable need is a question of fact and is up to the judge in each given case if a settlement is not possible. The law is clear: the financial obligations between a divorced couple should be ended as soon as possible. The judge must take into account all the facts and circumstances when making a decision.

Cohabitation would suggest that your former wife's "reasonable needs" should now be met by your former wife and her new partner, rather than by you. It doesn't always happen, say if the new partner is unable to provide for your former wife, or if there are other good reasons why the court decides that maintenance should continue for now. One example, although I don't think it applies in your case, could be if the new relationship was tenuous and your marriage had been lengthy, without the possibility of a clean break when it ended.

When two different homes are being maintained by a cohabiting couple, the judge still has to consider the issue of need and, where there is a need, the extent and term of maintenance. The judge would still take the existence of a new partner into account, even if that new partner is living elsewhere. The judge would also consider whether or not the recipient spouse was trying to pull the wool over the eyes of the paying spouse and the court.

Your argument certainly isn't new. It is routinely argued in court by paying spouses who are anxious to end their financial obligations. But it is difficult to say what will happen, without full knowledge of all the facts and finances. Please also note that when a paying spouse tries to end maintenance, the recipient spouse can sometimes make an application for capitalisation (a lump sum payment).

Regards,

Marilyn

Big money cases: dividing the assets

CASEBOOK

My client Mr M, aged 58, consulted me about the breakdown of his second marriage. He had just sold his business for a net sum of £18 million. He had inheritances from various family members, totalling £1 million. His pension, which he had no plans to draw down, was worth £1.5 million on top of that. A "golden handcuffs" clause in his contract required him to continue to work for the company for the next five years on an annual income of £200,000; with bonuses, he expected this to double. He and his wife owned a house worth £2 million. Total assets including the pension and excluding income, amounted to £22.5 million.

His first marriage had ended when he had fallen in love with his second wife, who was then his married PA. Within six months the PA had divorced her husband and married my client. Ten years later, this marriage was over too. She was now 48 and there were two children. The second wife demanded half of everything my client had and half his future income, including his bonuses. Was she right?

I was able to put my client's mind at ease, by telling him that this was going to be a "clean break" settlement; there was certainly sufficient capital to meet all his wife's claims. He had no need to worry about paying her any maintenance in the future. When I told him that I also thought his pension would remain untouched, he finally began to relax!

The question at hand was how much of the capital the wife would receive. In law she is entitled to share in all the assets, but should she share in assets he had before they married or assets received as an inheritance?

Fortunately for Mr M, he was already a wealthy man at the time of his second marriage. Had all his wealth been accumulated during his second marriage, his wife would certainly have been entitled to seek a 50:50 share of capital. But as a large part of his wealth was non-matrimonial, he had some strong arguments in his favour.

So how did it work out? First we looked at both parties reasonable needs.

The Duxbury Tables came out. The capitalised figure for his second wife's maintenance requirements formed part of her settlement, together with a payment for her rehousing and a claim for her share of the net proceeds of sale of the business based on the growth during the marriage.

Mrs M's solicitors put forward an astronomical budget, of almost £400,000, which we negotiated down after a helpful steer in that direction from the judge at the FDR. He took the view that her budget was purely aspirational. This is not uncommon.

However big or small the budget my tip is to care-fully check it and try and arrive at a figure that is reasonable. Many husbands shoot themselves in the foot by putting in a vast budget for themselves and then argue in vain the wife should receive less. Conversely they can put in a budget that is far too low for them, which thereby frees up their income for the wife! It's getting it just right that's the hard part.

In this case the wife's lawyers, acting very sen-sibly on the judge's advice, advised her to lower her income aspirations and to try and settle.

Following a compromise, a Duxbury income fig-ure of £150,000 was agreed. The wife received £8.5 million against a total sum of £22.5 million. With her payment she could comfortably rehouse and live elegantly for the rest of her life. Mr and Mrs M eventually left the FDR exhausted at the end of a long day – but both were relieved that the ordeal was finally over. The split was 62:38 in my clients favour.

When assets in such a medium-term "big money" mar-riage are divided, it is a difficult case to call. If the capital ex-ceeds the reasonable needs of both husband and wife, how should the surplus be allocated?

In cases where the assets have been earned during the marriage, the starting point is 50:50.

The client featured above, however, was well off before the

marriage took place. He had earned £18 million from the sale of his business, but estimated that the business was worth at least £7 million at today's values, prior to the marriage. Subtract (for the sake of argument) £7 million from £18 million. The net value for sharing could be £11 million. He also had his inheritances of £1 million and a pension, worth £500,000 in today's values at the start of the marriage, to exclude. We could thus argue that a substantial part of the capital, £8.5 million, was "non-matrimonial" and therefore should not be shared in the same way as the marital assets. We argued there were more than enough matrimonial assets to satisfy the wife's claims adequately.

The remaining assets were regarded as "matrimonial", being acquired during the marriage and available for sharing between the parties. The "matrimonial assets" totalled about £14 million and the "non-matrimonial" assets were about £8.5 million. This totalled £22 million.

In my client's case I couldn't predict with absolute certainty what the court would do, but thought that at least £7 million to start negotiations would be fair, which thus excluded our valuations of pre-marital asserts and the inheritance. The wife, on the other hand, was looking for nearer £11 million. Both parties still wanted to settle.

Would my suggested split be sufficient to cover the wife's reasonable needs, in accordance with the criteria set out in section 25 of the Matrimonial Causes Act 1973? Obviously the answer was yes - more than enough. We had to consider her income needs and other capital needs such as housing and furnishings. My client estimated his wife's true annual net income requirement at around £150,000.

In cases such as these, I use the Duxbury Tables to compute the capital payment needed to satisfy a spouse's income requirements for the rest of his or her life. For the case above, the Duxbury Tables suggested that a sum in the region of £3,727,000 would meet a lifetime income requirement of £150,000.

To that sum, there had to be added enough for a new house and other capital requirements. The grand total averaged out at less than the sharing figure of £7 million had produced. But the wife was also entitled to share in the success of the company during the marriage.

Therefore by cross-checking against her reasonable needs within the context of her marriage, the wife would receive more than she needed because in law, the sharing principle applies. No distinction is made between the homemaker and the breadwinner. That would not reduce the amount of the award, but if her needs produced a higher figure, the court would award her a greater sum. By following this method, the husband was still set to retain the larger part of his capital, plus his pension and continuing income.

The wife argued against a figure of £7 million being subtracted from the value of the business. She had a good point. There are a number of ways of arriving at the pre-marital value of a business, as any accountant will tell you. Each depends on its facts.

The hard part therefore was the negotiation, which involved give and take on both sides. The husband gradually increased his offer; the wife reduced hers. The wife of ten years was ultimately set to receive £8.5 million, which included the sum to be spent on rehousing. Costs were paid by each party out of their respective shares. The husband was left with £14 million and his future income intact. Neither party was anxious to test out their case in court, knowing that large sums of their money would be spent on barristers, solicitors and professional witnesses attributing their opinions of values to the assets.

This is an example of a deal done in a big money case, to which there is no "one size fits all" answer. Some would say the wife would have done better had she had fought in court. It's hard to say. Had the award been varied by a few million pounds either way, it would still have been regarded as what lawyers call "in the bracket".

The current form of judicial reasoning for these types of settlement is complicated and much criticised. Since White v White, all kinds of arguments have been developed to try and avoid a 50:50 share-out for the less wealthy spouse. Complex jurisprudence at the highest levels means that it is a challenge to advise a client caught up in this scenario who, from the outset, wants straight answers to straight questions. However if future legislation excludes non-matrimonial assets from the sharing principle in those cases where needs have been met (and all the indications suggest the wind is blowing that way) it should make calculations easier in these cases - although it may only reiterate what is presently happening in practice. For most of us, of course, it won't matter at all. Very few cases exist where there are surplus assets and even fewer involve eye-watering sums of money.

However if you do manage to reach a hard-fought deal at court, do remember that in all cases, once an agreement is signed or an order is made, it is notoriously difficult to overturn. This applies even when assets turn out to be worth far less or far more than previously estimated or less "safe" than you think. The exceptions tend to be cases involving fraud and that is very difficult to prove. Remember this when you are signing up to an agreement. Don't ever think to yourself that you will get a second chance. You won't. The court has closed its doors to those who "made a mistake" and valued an asset at more or less than it turned out to be worth. So if you are in doubt about concluding a deal, ask for more time to reflect. Don't be browbeaten. Consider also if you are getting enough of the copper-bottomed assets, or if you are being left with too much risk. Right now cash is king. A fair opponent won't mind waiting a day or so to allow you to sleep on it.

19: So What Do You Want to Know About Prenuptial Agreements?

I do not like the concept of prenuptial agreements, do not believe they are "socially necessary" and do not believe that they should be automatically legally binding. I would not have signed one myself, nor married anyone who asked me to as a precondition of marriage.

That said, I field a number of enquiries about prenups, both from clients who are due to marry and want to protect pre-owned or inherited assets, and clients who are due to divorce. The latter usually wish to know if their prenups will be upheld. The answer isn't always straightforward.

In 2010 a landmark decision was made by the Supreme Court in Radmacher v Granatino: a case involving a German heiress and her former husband, a Frenchman. The couple had signed a prenuptial agreement in Germany before moving to England. When they divorced, divorce proceedings were issued in England and the husband's legal team argued that although the prenuptial agreement would have been valid if the couple had divorced in Germany, it was not valid here. The Supreme Court judges decided that in this case, the German prenuptial agreement could be upheld. They ruled that, provided certain formalities are complied with, a prenup can hold "decisive" weight. In other words, prenups are now presumed binding unless they are deemed to be "unfair".

I suspect that the judges were also making a policy statement: *"England is no longer the divorce capital of the world"*. We gained this reputation a few years ago, when spectacular awards were made to the wives of a few wealthy men. Their cases made glamorous material for the press, put fear into the hearts of many rich husbands and hope into the hearts of their wives. Since then there have been more cases where a prenuptial agreement has been largely upheld, but the poorer party's needs have been met. It is expected that new legislation will be in that the same or similar form.

Q: Are prenuptial agreements worth the paper on which they are written?

A: Yes. It is a myth that prenups carry no weight in a court of law. When advising my clients about prenuptial agreements, I ask the following questions:

1. How soon before the wedding was it signed?

2. Was any pressure placed on the parties to sign it?

3. Was there any negotiation at all, or was the agreement imposed on one party?

4. Was there full and frank disclosure of the finances of both parties?

5. Did both parties receive legal advice?

6. Have both parties' needs been met in the agreement?

A prenuptial agreement is likely to be upheld if it was consensual and voluntary, not signed in haste, not clearly out of date (providing for future children, for example, and preferably including a review after a period of time) and properly drafted with full disclosure. A prenup is likely to be upheld if needs have been met – but it is important to note that this is not the same as meeting needs "generously" out of the available assets. For this reason, both parties should have received sound legal advice from separate lawyers before signing. Be warned: if you don't want to sign – don't.

Q: So what you are saying is, *"maybe"*. That's a bit of a cop-out, isn't it?

A: No, not really. In this country, the jurisdiction of the judge is unfettered when reaching a settlement. In my opinion, that remains the best system by far. The courts have the last word on the division of all matrimonial property.

Because prenups are not automatically binding, the party who wishes for an agreement to be upheld must mount the challenge. This allows the court to retain its right to act in pursuit of a fair result for both parties.

In the USA and in countries including Germany and South Africa, where prenuptial agreements are automatically binding, it is for the poorer spouse to mount the challenge. Unscrupulous spouses can insert clauses into these agreements to ensure that if a challenge is made, the payment is immediately reduced to nil. In such circumstances, the poorer spouse can come away with little or nothing.

CASEBOOK

Mrs H came to see me in tears. She produced a prenuptial agreement that she had signed the day before her wedding, 20 years previously. All she was to receive in the event of a divorce was £2,000. During the marriage, she had paid all her inheri-

---

tance of £150,000 into their home, which was still owned entirely by her husband. It was now worth £1.5 million. Her husband was a high earner and they had an elegant lifestyle. She told me that it was all superficial, and that she was desperately unhappy. The prospect of divorce and receiving only £2,000 had kept her chained in the marriage. She felt that she was now on the verge of a breakdown.

I was able to reassure her. I explained that the court would look at her needs and would look at a fair and reasonable settlement, based on fairly sharing the assets between them. Although all assets are available for sharing, the court may "ring fence" non-matrimonial assets, which are those assets acquired outside of the marriage. They might include an inheritance or gift.

In recent years parents of prospective brides and grooms have been coming to see me in increasing numbers, to ask about prenups. Many of these parents are wealthy, some are super-wealthy and others are not wealthy at all. What they share are concerns about what will happen if their children's marriages break down. They don't want any of their hard-earned cash to pass to the divorcing spouses, and they are determined to protect their money.

Similarly, people getting married for a second or third time wish to protect their assets. Many of them know that when older people get married, needs will increase as earning capacity can dwindle. They would prefer to see their estates going to their children. So they ask for protection.

This is understandable. However is it reasonable, or advisable, for a wealthy parent to expect a future son-in-law or daughter-in-law to enter into a prenuptial agreement? I'm not so sure. What is often overlooked is the effect of a prenuptial agreement on the marriage itself.

It is becoming commonplace to require a prenuptial agreement to be signed at least three weeks before the wedding. Yet by this time, the wedding arrangements have already been made. The guest list is in place, the honeymoon is booked, the dress purchased, the flowers, reception, food and drink all arranged... For the weaker party, worried about the legal consequences of jeopardising the commercial arrangements for the wedding, it is far easier to simply concede and sign.

Arguments have been made that the prenuptial agreement should form a "bridge" between civil and family proceedings, with automatic legal recognition of a prenup. However in commercial transactions, the parties are not emotionally tied. They negotiate at arm's length and, importantly, both stand to gain from the deal. In the case of a prenuptial agreement, the weaker party stands to lose and would do so twice over if a legal hurdle was put into place.

I also believe that in many cases, the existence of such an agreement can actually bring about a divorce. Consider the vulnerability of any newly married couple, working to make their marriage a success. Suppose they are showered with wealth by one side of the family. Then consider the effects of the imbalance that results if a prenuptial agreement is added to this equation. One party has the money; the other party is shackled to a piece of paper that – in theory – leaves him or her unable to ask the court to use its discretion and consider needs and entitlements in the normal way. They are married, but they do not have an equal footing within their marriage. Their attempt to forge a life together can only be hampered by such pressures. I have found that in many cases, the feeling of being "shackled" worsens over time. One way round this problem is to provide for a review after a fixed period.

If family members feel the need to protect their money, they could ring-fence it so that no outright gifts are made at all or until they are satisfied that the marriage will work. At Stowe Family Law we often advise parents on suitable trust structures and acquisitions of assets, loans and mortgages, in order to protect family money or assets. It isn't ideal and isn't necessarily tax effective either, but this is a practical option - although it is not usually welcomed by the parents who do want tax-effective forms of settlement. However it does mean that unwelcome and unpleasant pressure is not placed upon a young couple about to begin their life together, and it also means that the balance of power between them is not disturbed.

Q: I am asking my future wife to sign a prenuptial agreement, because I have been married before and don't want to be stung again! How can I do my best to ensure that it is upheld?

A: Ultimately, you may have to resort to litigation to "test" your agreement. As described above, the court will apply the test of fairness and what is reasonable between you. Many factors have been identified as pertinent in relation to a prenuptial agreement, ranging from duress, time, disclosure, independent and competent legal advice beforehand, to the provision for regular reviews and equality of bargaining power. If you want to do your best to make it stick, and I can certainly understand your desire to protect as much of your pre-acquired wealth as you can, I would recommend a deal that covers your future spouse's needs. They dont have to be generously assessed but equally, if they are too mean, the court might not approve of the arrangements. Where would your wife live? You could still own the property. How much income would she need? Would a lump sum be sufficient? Take advice from a lawyer who knows your circumstances.

Q: Is it true that the law is going to change?

A: It will happen. The Law Commission, which advises the government, is currently examining the legal status and enforceability of marital property agreements, including prenups. Any changes that are proposed and accepted will become effective in 2014 at the earliest. New legislation will legalise certain qualifying prenups and postnups (agreements made after marriage about a future divorce settlement) that meet a party's needs. In addition, it is likely that providing needs have been met, non-matrimonial assets will be legally removed from the shared "pot".

CASEBOOK

Mr J had worked hard all his life to make his

---

fortune. He didn't trust his son's judgment about his son's future wife. He permitted his son and the new wife to live rent-free in a beautiful house he owned on his estate. The son and his wife lived well through the father. However when it came to their divorce, the wife couldn't touch Mr J's wealth and the house remained his property. It was not an asset that belonged to his son and could not be taken into account in the divorce.

Mr J's judgment had proved correct. Interestingly the wife, on being advised that she would have little or no outright capital settlement, decided to stay in her marriage.

Dear Marilyn

I signed a prenuptial agreement in South Africa. It states that my wife would be entitled to very little by way of a financial settlement. It states that South Africa is to be the country where divorce proceedings take place. We do have children and of course I would fully support them. My wife and I are South African nationals but now living in England, although we retain a house in South Africa and go there during school holidays. What is your advice, because she keeps threatening to divorce me in England and screw me into the ground!

Bruce

Dear Bruce

Take advice immediately from a South African lawyer to find out if you can issue proceedings, even though you are both now virtually resident in England. I suspect you can. If you can issue proceedings in South Africa, I suggest you do so as soon as possible. Your wife may decide to proceed in this country and argue that the prenuptial agreement should not be upheld.

In contrast to European countries, the "first out of the starting blocks" argument to secure jurisdiction does not apply here. In your case, the court would have to decide which country has the greatest connection to the case. Given your respective connections with South Africa and that this is a South African prenuptial agreement which would have the force of law in South Africa, if you proceed first and the case goes ahead, I think the English court would decline to act.

Marilyn

20: Tracking Down Hidden Assets

It is not too difficult for anybody who has a basic understanding of personal finance to hide assets away in hard-to-trace accounts. Having a good solicitor on your side significantly raises the chances of unearthing these accounts, but the cost of finding them can take a sizeable chunk out of whatever sum is eventually recovered. This is why I stress the importance of finding out just what your partner is worth before it reaches this stage. Once a divorce gets into full swing, as it were, the atmosphere can become fraught. Your partner may be less than willing to divulge the whereabouts of every last penny. It isn't easy because not every spouse is willing to tell their other half what they are worth. What is more, any steps you do take must be legal. You cannot rummage through your spouse's personal papers without his or her consent. The court takes this very seriously and in some extreme cases, has imposed substantial costs orders.

You may think that this advice seems somewhat redundant. Would that your spouse had the funds and knowhow to stash away secret savings in the first place! Let me give you a couple of examples of wives who thought the same. Neither of them considered that their husbands were anything out of the ordinary when they came to see me, but within a few months the picture had changed completely.

CASEBOOK

Mrs C had been had been married for several

---

*years. Her husband ran a small shop selling gro-
ceries and, while they were comfortable, there was
nothing to indicate that he might have anything
hidden away. When Mrs C filed for divorce, we
carried out a company search at Companies House
just in case. It revealed that in addition to that small
corner shop, the husband had an extensive portfolio of properties and owned several supermarkets
in the area!*

*In another case, our client told us she thought that
her husband had one or two "private" accounts and
asked for our advice. She hadn't told him of her intention to divorce at that point, so we suggested
that we find out as much as was legally possible
about his financial situation before she did so. She
rooted around in the papers and documents in the
couple's shared study. As the couple ran a business together, she had always had access to these
files. With an expert eye, we then asked questions
about the destinations of some of the monies on the
bank statements. Our forensic accountancy team
unearthed various bank accounts held by her husband in the Channel Islands, which he had not disclosed on his Form E.*

*When the case began, her husband declared UK
assets of around £100,000. But with the help of
these earlier enquiries, we were able to prove the
existence of assets running into millions. We began*

our work by analysing the bank statements that he had disclosed. We secured court orders so that we could access trust documentation, additional bank statements, credit card statements and telephone records. We investigated his business activities in some detail to put a value on his business, and discovered that he was trading in various countries. The internet is a powerful tool. We built up a picture that was entirely different from the one that he had presented to the court. Armed with the information we had gathered, we were able to obtain a "search and seize" order of his flat and took possession of his personal computer, from which we had permission to download files, under the very strict terms of the court order. It took a long time and it was an expensive gamble, but it was worth it. Mrs S received a handsome settlement.

While these cases are extraordinary and very much the exception rather than the rule, they do show the importance of carrying out the appropriate checks before agreeing a settlement. Even if your partner has been with the same company for 20 or 30 years and could never have amassed significant savings, he or she could still be worth a good deal more than you think.

A note of caution

Enquiries must kept in proportion to the likely eventualities. As much as you may wish a secret fortune upon your spouse, in reality such surprises are rare. Don't squander your money on investigations that will amount to little.

Clients often wish to undertake their own detective work. I should stress again, however, that DIY is not recommended. We actively discourage clients from accessing data which, without a court order, would be accessed unlawfully. Such actions could render them liable to civil and criminal legal proceedings. These days even seemingly innocuous activities, such as searching through your spouse's private belongings for financial information, taking possession of his or her papers, photocopying them and trying to hand them to your lawyers - all apparently reasonable when you tell yourself that all is fair in love and war –fall within this bracket. The Court may refuse to admit the information obtained in this way and make costs orders against you for breach of the law. *See Chapter 29: Other Pitfalls, and How to Avoid Them* for further information about illegal activities and the potential penalties.

Furthermore, non-specialists may find it difficult to isolate the relevant facts from the available information. "Exciting" revelations can turn out to be anything but. Marked suspicion carries little weight in the eyes of the law: if a court is to find in your favour, hard evidence is required.

Overall, I would recommend that you are cautious about everything you do. Take advice first. Some judges require a good deal of persuasion. It can be that the more spectacular the case is, the greater the challenges and scepticism are. Remember the adage that all that glitters is not gold.

How a forensic accountant can help you

Settlements and payment terms require good negotiation skills. At Stowe Family Law we are assisted by an in-house forensic accountancy department.

The team:

- Specialises in tracking down hidden assets in the UK and around the world.
- Works "backwards" to unearth as much information as possible about your partner's financial situation.
- Can provide immediate advice about the likely scale and nature of a case. With access to Companies House and global databases, our accountants download information, analyse it immediately and advise us where to concentrate our efforts.
- Can provide advice about the likely value of a client's business for the purpose of a divorce. This is useful because business values may be artificially inflated or deflated by the client, for a variety of reasons.

It means that when clients come to see us, there is no frustrating wait for financial information before we can advise on tactics. Instead, we can begin work immediately. This is particularly pertinent when we have to consider an asset-freezing order against a client's spouse. In such a case, time is of the essence.

On occasions, a client's understanding of a spouse's financial situation does not match the reality. With a forensic accountant as an advisor, the client can be given a swift, measured opinion at the first or second interview. There are plenty of excellent forensic accountants around the country, and you may find it worth your while to consult one. Not everyone realises that in divorce they can play an important role.

Disclosing your hidden assets

What if you are the one with bank accounts in Switzerland? If Her Majesty's Revenue and Customs find out, you may be prosecuted. Your marriage fails and divorce proceedings begin. What do you do? Dare you disclose the information?

This is a subject about which I write frequently on my blog. One popular post focused upon the quandary of a man known as "Mr K", in a 2009 case called R V K. Mr K disclosed information about his offshore assets in his Form E. In a subsequent meeting in October 2001, attended by his solicitor and his wife's solicitor, he made incriminating statements about the nature of the assets. He admitted that he had received a large sum of money from Switzerland, which he had not declared for tax purposes.

At a second meeting in April 2002, which was held "without prejudice", proposals for settlement were discussed. During this meeting the husband noted that there was a "major tax problem" and a "real chance" that he could go to jail. An "informer" then supplied the Form E and records of the meetings to Her Majesty's Revenue & Customs. As the husband had predicted, he was prosecuted.

Were his Form E and statements admissible as evidence? The judge found they were. The Court of Appeal took a different view, however, delivering an impressively reasoned decision. It was held that Mr K had no choice in law but to tell the truth, the whole truth and nothing but the truth, on oath, in his financial disclosure within the divorce proceedings.

The information was therefore given under compulsion. The Court of Appeal found that it would be a breach of the European Convention on Human Rights to take material that had been compulsorily given in divorce proceedings, for use in criminal proceedings. In this the court followed other cases, most notably that of Ernest Saunders in the Guinness trial in 1991. The European Court of Human Rights later found that Saunders had been denied a fair trial: his human rights had been breached because information that he had been compelled to give to Department of Trade and Industry inspectors had subsequently been used against him at his criminal trial.

As for Mr K: were the statements that he had made in both meetings inadmissible? The Court of Appeal held that in the first meeting, Mr K had orally amplified the contents of his Form E with additional information. Otherwise he would have been compelled to provide the same information in written answers. The information was therefore given under compulsion and was inadmissible

In the second meeting in April 2002, when he had made the incriminating statement about going to jail, the Court of Appeal found that he was not protected, even though the meeting was held "without prejudice". The Court held that the use of the term "without prejudice" was powerful and that in civil matters, it would likely give protection to those who spoke frankly in meetings. In criminal cases, however, the interests of public policy outweigh the right to speak frankly and conclude private deals.

In summary: if the fullest incriminating information is given by a spouse by way of disclosure and if he has no choice but to give this information, including bank statements, it cannot be used in a subsequent prosecution. This is because the person providing the information has been compelled to do so and has no choice.

Dear Marilyn

I divorced my husband four years ago and received a modest settlement. I have since learned that he had a "secret" bank account where, I am told, he put more than £200,000 from the sale of his share options. During our divorce, he said those share options were worthless! Am I entitled to anything?

Katie

Dear Katie,

This is certainly one for the lawyers to argue over! Were the shares worthless at the time of the divorce and did their value rise to £200,000 only at a later date? If so, you have an uphill task. Or were they worth £200,000 at the time of your divorce and therefore was he misleading or even defrauding you? What did he know and what can you prove? Four years is a long time and the court will be reluctant to reopen a court order unless there are very compelling reasons to do so, such as fraud. On balance, I think you should investigate further.

> *Your solicitor may write to your former hus-*
> *band and ask him to produce information about his*
> *share options. If your former husband refuses to*
> *comply, you can apply to set aside the order on the*
> *basis that the court was deliberately misled as to*
> *the financial situation. It is very difficult to set aside*
> *a court order if you do not possess clear facts to*
> *support your hunch. If you do make an application,*
> *this is a lengthy, difficult and expensive process, so*
> *weigh up the potential benefits before proceed-*
> *ing and incurring costs. If he makes you an offer it*
> *could be worth taking. This is all-or-nothing type*
> *litigation so the risks are high.*
>
> *Marilyn*

What if you suspect fraud?

When financial cases are bitterly contested, there can be allegations of non disclosure and even fraud against spouses whose disclosed incomes and assets are less than expected.

If your spouse has supervised the family finances, you may know little about the couple's overall financial standing. So if your spouse is creative and anticipates a divorce, they may try and divest themselves of assets in order to produce a relative-ly modest balance sheet. In such a situation, what can you do?

I will be blunt: perhaps your expectations are unrealistic. Perhaps you cannot accept what is there in black and white, because your emotions have clouded your judgment. Or per-haps your suspicions are well-placed, but proving them is another matter. What if the evidence rests in another solicitor's drawer? Is it possible to obtain the crucial file?

Take the following as an example; in my experience, it isn't an uncommon scenario.

A husband wishes to increase an asset portfolio that, on divorce, will be split. He doesn't want to pass up a terrific deal; equally, he is determined that his soon-to-be ex-wife should not benefit. He decides to have a nominee acquire the asset for him. This nominated representative may be a relative, a company or even an offshore trust. The husband gives explicit instructions to his commercial solicitors as to how the transaction is to proceed, revealing that he is ultimately set to benefit. The nominee also instructs the solicitors, and the asset is duly acquired. In such a case, all parties concerned are fully aware that the husband is the overall beneficiary. However, his actions will minimise his wife's claims against him. The wife guesses what is going on, but she can't be sure. She doesn't know if the transaction has taken place, what it is or how much money it involves. She knows her husband, however, and is convinced something is up.

This is fraud. If it ever came to light, the couple's marital settlement could be set aside and the husband could be prosecuted for perjury.

What can she do?

This is a tricky one. She could ask questions of the third party with the assistance, if necessary, of a subpoena and a hearing before a court. However she would not necessarily get the answers she seeks as she does not have power to "cross examine" the third party. She has to decide if the cost of proceeding and the risk of paying the third party costs are worth it.

If there is clear, incontrovertible evidence of fraudulent collusion and asset acquisition, she could try and join the third party into the proceedings. However without clear and convincing evidence this is a very risky and expensive procedure.

She could make a complaint to the police, but how seriously they would take the complaint is a matter for them.

Even though there is an ongoing duty of full and frank disclosure in financial cases in family law until a court order is made, the husband could therefore get away with it. The powers of the family law court are not the same as those of the police, who are in a position to obtain information through simple, unopposed court orders. The transaction described above should clearly have been disclosed, with the court and the man's wife made aware of the position.

So could the court order disclosure of the relevant files held by law firms on behalf of the husband and his best friend? The answer is no, at least not all of the files. The instructions and advice given on the files are protected by professional privilege - and these are exactly what the wife is trying to obtain.

The courts preserve the right of a client to take legal advice free from outside scrutiny. Because of this, all instructions and advice remain strictly confidential.

Someone giving instructions to a solicitor and taking advice can be assured that a confidence will remain a closely guarded secret. This is as it should be. But it means that the wife cannot get her hands on the information and prove the fraud.

This may seem unfair and circuitous. How could the wife prove fraud without access to the file? But bear in mind that solicitors are Officers of the Court: they cannot mislead the court and present a false financial picture of a client.

Sometimes the client tries to pull off this type of deception through the commercial department at his or her own family law solicitors. Solicitors' professional obligations to the court should prevent this happening and they could not continue to act in the family law proceedings if their client refused to tell the truth. I had a case once in which we were misled by the commercial department of a firm, with the family lawyer in the same firm unaware of what was going on. When he did find out, the firm stopped acting for the husband.

21: How To Keep Your Costs Down

The reason why most people decide not to instruct solicitors is because of the cost. Sometimes it is not worth it, because the value of the assets do not warrant expensive legal fees. Sometimes people prefer to save money and spend it on themselves. My view is that a good lawyer who does a good job will help you come out on top. But it makes sense to try and contain your legal fees. Sometimes legal fees can increase with or without your help.

Five ways to increase your divorce costs

1. **Sticking your head in the sand.** It is pointless to duck the question of costs just because you don't want to know the answer. My advice is the same every time: face it, deal with it and then get on with the case, to achieve your desired result. It would be a great mistake to remain uninformed. You need to understand from your solicitor when you will be billed and how you are going to pay the bill. Don't wait until the bill drops on your mat. Remember: you and your solicitor are working together in a commercial partnership.

2. **It's complicated.** Your financial affairs are complex and specialists must be drafted in. Likewise, it is important to note that a case may end up costing more than originally expected. Unforeseen circumstances can and do arise.

3. **Insisting your solicitor tackles the smallest details.** Every additional complication that a solicitor has to investigate or settle inevitably ends up on the bill.

While you may believe that your spouse's behaviour outside the family home is worth complaining about, is it really worth increasing costs to prove the point?

4. **Litigation misconduct.** A bitter spouse can decide to argue even the most trivial details in court as a way of "making him (or her) suffer". While one can understand the motives, such an approach can and often does backfire. Ultimately, the person's assets may be eaten up by legal costs, leaving them with little. Even if this doesn't happen, the court could ask them to pay the other party's costs because of this obstinate, bloody-minded attitude. This shouldn't deter anyone who has a reasonable claim from pressing home his or her case, but it should serve as a warning against litigation for the sake of revenge.

5. **Believing that the richer party has to pay the costs.** This is a dangerous mistake to make. The general rule is that each side pays their own costs. This rule can present a significant challenge for the poorer party, who risks being "outgunned" by the wealthier spouse. The answer is to maintain a commercial approach at all times.

How to lower your costs

1. **Move swiftly.** If your divorce drags on, costs will mount. Prepare details of respective finances with supporting documentation as soon as possible. Find a reputable solicitor who will provide a good steer on the outcome of your case and an estimate of likely costs. Issuing an application to court timetables the case and can save

legal costs in the long run. If a divorce is imminent and you live overseas or have overseas connections, immediate action is essential – legislation and likely financial settlements vary from country to country. We have dealt with cases in which proceedings have been issued in different countries, literally minutes apart. Within the EU, as previously noted, for the party filing last there is no second chance. If you delay filing papers, you risk disabling your case – and wallet – from the start. _See chapter 15 for further information._

Get your timing right. If at all possible, don't separate just before the end of a tax year, as you will have little time in which to consider the most tax-efficient arrangements. For example, you may incur a bill for capital gains tax at a time when your finances are particularly vulnerable. In the eyes of HM Revenue & Customs, transfers of assets such as property and company shares result in no immediate capital gains tax liability, as long as they take place in the tax year during which you separate.

2. **Make interim arrangements for bills.** Even if your divorce proceeds swiftly, it will be months before a final settlement. Don't ignore debts and decisions about who will pay them. If you cannot agree, you can apply to the court for an interim order, but this may not be cost effective. Alternatively, see if the bank will help until the house is sold.

3. **Consider using a collaborative lawyer, mediator or arbitrator.** Alternative forms of dispute resolution are becoming more popular, in part because legal

fees can be relatively low. Spouses sit around a "negotiating table" with collaborative lawyers, a mediator or an
arbitrator, and discuss the issues. What all these methods share is that they aim to agree on a fair outcome for
both parties and thrash out a deal, while keeping the
couple out of court. With lawyers charging by the hour,
fees can mount if negotiating is prolonged. _See chapter
8 for further information._

4. **Keep valuing assets.** Keep valuing assets until the
   case is sorted, especially if it's taking time. Know the full
   value of what you are settling for, particularly pensions.

5. **Cash is king.** This is especially true when the economy
   is gloomy, but remember, other assets can go up and
   down in value.

6. **Avoid Mesher orders.** A Mesher order postpones
   the sale of the marital home until a specified event takes
   place. It originated in 1980, when the Court of Appeal
   permitted a wife to remain in the marital home with
   one child until the child's 17th birthday, or until further
   order of the court. Such orders were popular during the
   last recession, when there was often insufficient capital
   to rehouse a newly divorced mother and her children.
   The difficulties surfaced when the houses came to be
   sold. In many cases, the mother discovered that despite
   inflation, there was still insufficient equity in her share
   to enable her to buy another property. In some cases,
   the woman was left worse off, because her reduced time
   left in the workplace meant she was unable to raise a
   mortgage. In some cases, the former husband was none
   too pleased to find that his share of the house was sub-

ject to capital gains tax. In the current financial climate, with houses difficult to sell and mortgages difficult to obtain, Mesher orders are coming back into fashion. On balance, I would avoid them, if at all possible. It may well be preferable to downsize and own 100 per cent of a new home, than to own 66 per cent of a more expensive property that may someday have to be sold.

7. **Know what to do if your spouse goes bankrupt.** Don't be blind to this possibility. If you suspect your spouse is going to declare bankruptcy, make sure your solicitor gets you into court and obtains a court order as soon as possible. If the worst happens, you may still be entitled to stay in the family home for a year and you can still claim your share of that property's equity. Some spouses go bankrupt deliberately, to avoid debts and payment of any financial settlements. It could backfire. In one startling case reported in 2009, a husband declared bankruptcy despite earning £100,000 a year and driving a Rolls-Royce Phantom. His bankruptcy was later annulled, and he was ordered to pay his wife £1m.

What to do if you can't pay your solicitors' fees

In family law, "no win no fee" systems are illegal. So are the systems whereby the solicitor charges a "percentage of the value of the case at the end of the case".

Legal aid has been all but abolished. However if you are in financially straitened circumstances, you do have a number of options.

Divorce loans. A bank may help you out. It is possible to negotiate a loan so your solicitor is paid as usual during the case. Some banks will fund your costs if you undertake to re-pay them out of your settlement. They may also agree to "roll up" the interest payments into the final payment, so that no repayment is made before the case is over. This is not an un-usual procedure, and there are a few banks that specialise in this type of funding. Your solicitor will be able to advise you.

At the time of writing, the economic climate means that such loans are not as easy to come by as they were. However they are still available from certain banks. If you need one, make an appointment with your bank manager and request assistance.

Court order. It is possible to apply to the court for an or-der to make funds available, out of your spouse's income or by what is, effectively, a capital distribution. There are ingenious ways of doing this, such as an award of backdated mainte-nance, but note that the income or capital has to be available in the first place.

The court will not make an order for payment of legal costs out of the other party's income unless there is absolutely no other way of having the costs paid. Evidence must be pro-duced to that effect. That must include the solicitors of the applicant party refusing to enter into a "Sears Tooth" agree-ment. Shortly it may also be possible for the court to award an "interim lump sum".

Sears Tooth agreement. This is a deed signed by client and solicitor. When such an agreement is made, the solicitor agrees to fund the case. The client assigns part of the capital settlement to the solicitors to cover the client's bill of costs, as agreed or assessed by the court.

If such an agreement is signed by the client and witnessed

by an independent solicitor, it will be upheld by a court if a dispute about it arises in the future. A lump sum settlement awarded in a divorce can be legally assigned in this way.

Once signed, the Sears Tooth agreement must be disclosed to the court and to the other party in the case.

Not many solicitors will take on such agreements. It is a gamble for them, especially if the case itself poses a risk. Furthermore, based on the agreement the solicitors must fund the disbursements in the case. These include court fees, surveyors' fees and barristers' fees. If anything goes wrong, then the solicitors will be left out of pocket.

However, there are times when it is the only way forward. Don't be afraid to ask! If the client has no choice, the solicitors may feel they have no choice. I've been there.

Part VI:
How To Do Your Best
For Your Children

22: You, Your Children and the Law

The welfare of children is the arguably the most important area of divorce law. Unfortunately, it is also an area of law plagued by conflict, heartache and rage. The failings of family courts are trumpeted in the newspapers, and fathers' rights groups have noisily protested the "unfairness" of the current system.

With so much at stake, this is always going to be a contentious area. To put your children first, both of you must be reasonable, prepared to compromise and prepared to think of what is best for the children, not what is best for you.

From time to time, one comes across an intransigent person who is incapable of objectivity when considering what is best for the child. In such cases, the courts are there to assist – and later in this section, we will take a closer look at what they can do. On the whole, however, parents can usually agree periods when the children are to see both of them and on the whole they can reach agreement about where the children are to be based.

You may not like your partner, but a child's view of their parent will be different. He or she will have love and trust for that person, capable of transcending even the most dreadful scenes that may have been witnessed. A child prevented from seeing a parent they still love will eventually turn that resentment against the one trying to enforce the unenforceable. In the end, reasonableness pays!

The courts are there if reasonable agreement between partners cannot be reached. Specialist lawyers can become involved and the Family Court Welfare Service, however strained the system, is also available.

It is important to emphasise that with regard to children, no order is ever permanent. With this in mind, there should be no reason why parties cannot reach a reasonable and sensible compromise, agreeing arrangements which are in the best possible interests for their children.

The following chapters, which concern the role of children during their parents' divorce, have been authored with the assistance of Stowe Family Law colleagues who have established excellent reputations in this field. They include solicitors Rachel Baul and Stephen Hopwood, who heads our Children's Department at Stowe Family Law and has three young children of his own.

An overview of the law

- The needs and welfare of the child are paramount. The child comes first in any decision, parents second and others a relatively distant third.
- The court can make any order in relation to a child. The court can make no order, when appropriate.
- No order in relation to a child is permanent. An order may be altered or discharged if the circumstances of the child alter.

• Once a child of divorcing parents comes under the umbrella of the court, this remains the position until the child becomes an adult. If ever there is a problem the court is the ultimate arbiter.

The key to the law and the approach of the court is that parents have responsibilities towards children and not rights over them. This phrase has been repeated to me by some very experienced judges.

Truth and fiction

There are always plenty of reports, rumours and dreadful stories in circulation, so before we go any further, let's debunk some of the common myths.

MYTH: The children will have to appear in court.

FALSE. They will not - although the views of older children may be sought.

MYTH: The court always favours the mother.

FALSE. This may have been so in the past, but increasing numbers of children are residing permanently with their fathers. The court considers what is best for the child in each individual case. The Government is shortly to introduce new legislation, which will provide for the desirability of joint but not shared parenting, provided it is safe for the child. The welfare of the child is always paramount.

MYTH: One parent gets custody; one parent must give it up.

FALSE. The concept of "custody" was abolished by the Children Act 1989, as was "access". Instead, both parents retain "responsibility" for their children.

The children will reside with one parent or may reside with both on a split basis if that is appropriate. They will have "contact" with their parents too. This used to be called "access".

MYTH: If a parent does not pay maintenance, his or her contact rights may be affected.

FALSE. You are not permitted to cite finance (or the lack of it) as a valid reason for reduced contact. This can work for or against the parent, depending on who is paying and who is receiving the payments.

MYTH: Rock the boat, and you will be looked upon unkindly.

FALSE. If you are not happy with arrangements made for contact, a court order can regulate the arrangement. Delay may be disastrous and can be cited as evidence that the status quo is acceptable.

Parental responsibility: what it means

The legal position is simple. If they are or were married to one another, both parents have parental responsibility. If an unmarried father has been named on a birth certificate completed after 2003, he has parental responsibility. If you have adopted a child, you have parental responsibility.

Parental responsibility allows you to apply for a passport on your child's behalf, and gives you the right to have a say in the following:

- Where your child lives.
- Where your child goes to school.
- Any medical treatment received by your child.
- Any decisions made with regard to religion and religious

upbringing.

Parental responsibility lasts until your child is 18, and allows you to take decisive action in emergency situations – seeking emergency medical treatment, for example.

The Children Act 1989

I would like to take a closer look at the Children Act 1989, which introduced the concept of parental responsibility. I believe that if you are a parent and you are getting divorced, you would be wise to acquaint yourself with the Act's contents. They have a role to play in your child's future, and therefore your future too.

The Children Act 1989 states that when the court determines any question relating to the upbringing of a child, the child's welfare shall be the court's paramount consideration. This is known as the Welfare Principle and it will determine any contested proceedings made under section 8 of the Children Act.

When applying the Welfare Principle, there is a checklist of factors which must be taken into consideration by the court. These are as follows:

1. **The ascertainable wishes and feelings of the child concerned (considered in light of his age and understanding);**
2. **The child's physical, emotional and educational needs;**
3. **The likely effect on the child of any change in circumstance;**
4. **The child's age, sex, background and any characteristics of the child which the Court consid-**

ers relevant;

5. **Any harm that the child has suffered or is at risk of suffering;**

6. **How capable each of the child's parents and any other person in relation to whom the Court considers the question relevant is of meeting the child's needs;**

7. **The range of powers available to the Court under the Children Act 1989 in the proceedings in question.**

This last factor is to encourage the court to consider every option available to it, which includes not making any order at all if that would be better for the child. In other words, the court will not make an order unless it can be demonstrated that there is a positive need to do so, and that the order will benefit the child.

There are four different types of orders which can be made, and these are as follows:

1. **Residence order.** This determines with whom a child will live. A shared residence order can be made, determining that the child's residence is with more than one person (see below). This does not always mean that the children's time will be divided evenly between each parent, but there needs to be some substantial split of time.

2. **Contact order.** There are occasions when a contact order, defining the time that the children will spend with a non-resident parent, is appropriate. One parent may not be able to manage the times needed to form a successful shared residence order, or that parent may

simply wish to have a traditional arrangement imposed upon their lives. A contact order requires the person with whom the child lives to make the child available to have contact with the other person named in the order. The other person is usually the non-resident parent, although a contact order can extend to other people such as grandparents. The contact can be direct - for example spending time with the child, including overnight stays - or indirect contact such as letters.

3. **Prohibited steps order.** This orders that no steps can be taken by a parent in meeting their parental responsibilities. One example would be an order preventing a parent from taking a child out of the jurisdiction.

4. **Specific issue order.** This gives directions to determine a specific question, which has arisen in connection with any aspect of parental responsibility. For example, such an order could determine the school to be attended by the child, or whether a child should undergo a particular operation.

In the case of prohibited steps orders and specific issue orders, one parent makes an application and the matter is heard before a judge. There may be further hearings; ultimately, the judge will make decisions about any remaining issues that cannot be agreed.

Deciding residence options and rights of contact

As families move further into the 21st century, old beliefs about parents' roles and responsibilities are changing. It was only a few years ago that judges would follow the basic principle that the father was the breadwinner and the mother looked after the children. The children were expected to remain living with the mother, who would certainly make the day-to-day decisions, and perhaps the decisions of greater importance too.

Then a shift occurred. There was a groundswell of opinion that a father being "afforded" time with his children was neither helpful, nor meeting the children's needs. Fathers, along with families in mediation, were asking for more flexible and inclusive arrangements. Leading counsel in London and the judiciary began to refer to "parenting time" and the concept that children cannot be properly parented by each parent if one of those parents sees them only at weekends. For example, how was each parent to engage with the school?

From this, the **shared residence order** was born. The concept was not new but had previously been restricted to those families who could agree on a way forward. Judges had felt that a shared residence order would only work if the parties were in agreement. The logic then changed and it was considered that such an order was even more relevant in cases when the parents could not agree. If they could agree, then what was the need for a shared residence order in any event?

The courts, even at a local level, have become far more willing to consider shared residence. It has to be based on the usual factors being considered in the welfare checklist, but generally these reflect what was happening previously. After all, many of today's fathers have a relatively hands-on approach to their children's upbringing.

CASEBOOK

Some years ago, Mr A came to see me about his wife. He was a consultant at a hospital. She was a medical researcher at a university. One day the wife announced that the marriage had gone stale, and that she wished to "move on". The couple both worked extremely long hours, and shared the care of their three children with a live-in nanny. The nanny had been with the family since the birth of their youngest child eight years previously.

Mr A felt that he had made considerable sacrifices for their children. He had declined lucrative private work, to better assist with childcare arrangements. He described how his wife had spent the previous evening with a "girlfriend" at a pop concert, while he had stayed at home to babysit.

From a legal perspective, the case seemed relatively straightforward. I advised him that there was no reason why a shared childcare arrangement could not continue as before, but from two homes. I did point out that if the nanny went to live with the mother, it was likely that the children would spend more time away from their father.

The finances could also be split equally, as both husband and wife earned similar incomes and were likely to reside in similar properties. The couple's pension arrangements were slanted in the husband's favour, but this was unlikely to make any significant difference. Both parties had healthy parents, so inheritance prospects were not relevant. Mr A would probably have to pay agreed child support and contribute equally to school fees.

On the face of it, there were no major problems. A few days later Mr A telephoned to arrange another appointment. He had discovered that his wife was conducting an affair with a female work colleague.

This situation is not uncommon and the law does not differentiate between same sex and heterosexual relationships to any great degree. It is always difficult to advise clients when a third party is involved, particularly the perceived impact on the children. In this case, Mr A decided that he was opposed to the idea of his children living under the same roof with two women.

It was likely that at some stage, the court would give the go-ahead for the children to reside with the mother and her new partner. The court does not differentiate between same sex relationships and heterosexual relationships. However, it was important to tread carefully. Although a case such as this, with clashing viewpoints, illustrates the challenges sometimes faced by lawyers, it is never my function as a lawyer to make moral judgments. Rather, I help clients to arrange acceptable settlements. Acting on my advice and what he felt to be his children's best interests, Mr A rethought this plans.

The nanny agreed to stay with him and he was able to reduce his working hours, so he could demonstrably become a full-time carer for the children. He made a claim for residence of the children and suggested a pattern of contact with their mother, which would not involve them staying overnight with her and her new partner for the foreseeable future. He looked to his wife for child support.

Following negotiations, we settled. Mr A bought out his wife for one third of the agreed equity in the property on a "clean break" basis, with no comebacks on either side. She is contributing maintenance payments. She pays more towards school fees; he pays the nanny. The children remain in the family home with their father and the nanny, and are slowly adjusting to the trauma of their mother's departure and her new relationship. At some point the children will stay with their mother and her new partner. Both parents have taken positive steps for the sake of their children, who are also being assisted by supportive teaching staff at their schools.

Will Mr A ever forgive his former wife? I think it unlikely. Some time afterwards I heard he had remarried. He married the nanny.

CAFCASS

If residence and contact decisions cannot be agreed upon

or are not working, either parent can apply for a court order. Usually this is to determine residence and contact. In most cases, the process unfolds as follows:

1. Faced with competing demands, a judge will often call upon the Court Welfare Service (CAFCASS). This is not a part of social services, but is there to provide advice and to report to the court.

2. A CAFCASS officer will visit you and the other parent to discuss the issues and will then make recommendations to the court. The officer will speak to you and will most likely see the children, but unless they are of reasonable age - 10 upwards, as a guide - will not speak to them directly. The officer will then draw up a report, focusing upon the best interests of the child and considering the comments of both parents.

3. You are not bound to accept the officer's recommendations, but they are for the judge to consider and will carry great weight. In the majority of cases with which I deal, parents do reach an agreement which is in the best interests of their child, even though it may go against their own personal desires.

Haircuts and day-to-day developments

Earlier in this chapter I described various court orders, including prohibited steps orders and specific orders. It is your right to seek a court order if you believe it is in the best interests of your child. I recommend, however, that you pick and choose your battles very carefully. A court order is a double-edged sword that imposes a duty on both parents. It also increases the temperature and the likelihood of a situation that neither one of you can forget nor forgive. If at all possible, avoid the courts.

Whatever the result of financial negotiations, you will be forever linked to your former partner through the children. That is surely worth a long pause for reflection. Your children will need joint financial and practical decisions made for them, for years to come.

There are likely be 101 minor issues on which you wish to take a stand. Ideally, you will want to discuss these issues amicably and sensibly. If that cannot be, it is possible that before long, solicitors will be communicating about when the children should have their hair cut! Clearly, such developments are to be avoided.

Try and avoid conflict over each and every small issue that crops up. Save your energy for bigger challenges. One solution that has worked well for a number of our clients is to say nothing. Instead they jot down issues in small notebooks, which are then put with each child's things at the handover.

A sample entry:

12.01.13 - Sam has a cold. Please give him Calpol every four hours. He now refuses to eat chips.

And in return: *13.01.13 - I have given Sam his Calpol. He had fish fingers for his tea. In the park he cut his knee when he fell – Savlon applied.*

This measure may seem trivial and unnecessary, but it can eliminate opportunities for conflict and misunderstanding. When relations are at such a low ebb, can you imagine having a rational discussion about a cut knee?

Holidays

The approach of school holidays can give rise to numerous problems concerned the time that each parent spends with the children. Divorce lawyers are beset by anxious queries. Can I take my children abroad? If so, for how long? Do I need consent? What if (s)he refuses?

The obvious solution is to sit down and talk with your former partner. This is easier said than done, but it is the cheapest and quickest way of reaching agreement. Unfortunately, all too often sensible conversations and compromises do not happen until the courts intervene. Quite why this is so I have never been able to understand. I am frequently approached by people who are prepared to spend an awful lot of money arguing about whether or not their children can go on that two-week holiday to Spain.

Under the provisions of the Children Act a parent with a residence order can take a child abroad for 28 days without needing the other parent's consent. Usually there is no residence order and the parties have to agree. If the matter cannot be resolved between the parties or by solicitors in negotiation, there may be an emergency application to the court and a judge will decide.

The judge may ask the following questions:
• Will the children be looked after adequately?
• Are the arrangements sensible?
• If an emergency arises, will the children be safe?

If the answers are all *"yes"*, then the holiday is likely to take place. Whether or not the children will enjoy the trip is often the last consideration of the warring parents, but it will be foremost in the judge's mind.

What to expect if you are a lone parent

I am often asked to advise parents who have not married their partners. They need to know the financial settlements they can expect for themselves and their children when co-habitation breaks down.

The length and nature of the couple's relationship is generally of little relevance. After all, a child born after a one night stand has the same needs and dependency as a child born after parents have cohabited for years.

When one party is wealthy, the arrangements often follow these lines:

- The parties should have broadly comparable homes. Even if the father enjoys greater financial resources than the mother, for example, their children are entitled to be raised by both parties in circumstances that bear a relationship to the wealthier parent's current resources and standard of living.
- This does not mean that in such cases, the mother would own the property. Instead it would be purchased by and owned by the father, and would revert back to him when the children became adults or finished their full time education.
- If the man is sufficiently wealthy, the wife could also be entitled to a "carer's allowance" (much like spousal maintenance). A lump sum, to cover the provision of a car and furnishings for the house may also be provided.

• Child support is payable.

CASEBOOK

Some of the cases with which I become involved strike me as "entrapment". I can recall one wealthy client, Mr W, who had to deal with a paternity suit from a Russian nightclub hostess after a one night stand. He had been wined and dined in a London club and, having drunk too much, had picked up the stunning woman. Following unprotected sex, the woman announced that she was pregnant - and paternity tests would later confirm that he was the father. Mr W was unlucky. Before the child was even born he was faced with the mother's applications for housing, maintenance and capital.

Mr W wanted to protect himself against any future comebacks. He agreed to provide funds to enable mother and child to live in a modest house that she would own, but on the basis that there would be no child support and no further claims against him. Any future claims would be offset against the equity in the house. The client decided to have no relationship at all with his child, and the matter ended peaceably. Perhaps in years to come, the child will wish to learn more about his millionaire father - and who would blame him? In law, however, this type of "clean break" arrangement is far from typical.

A note on names

We are often asked about children's names. You should know that typically, these should not be changed without agreement from both parents. This rule of thumb applies when the parents are married or divorced, or if the parents did not marry but the father has signed the birth certificate. If you wish to change a child's name but know that the proposed change will be contested, you should apply to the court.

Tempting as it is to revert to a maiden name or family name without that agreement, it is severely frowned upon by the court and they may even order that the name is changed back. This includes the name used upon the school roll. The court views a child's name as fundamental to his or her identity. Sudden and controversial name changes do not sit well with judges.

In short, it is your duty to work with the other parent for the best of their children, even during difficult times. Nothing can be more emotional or potentially destructive than proceedings regarding children, but approach the issue as a conflict and that is what will happen. Instead be firm, put your child at the centre of the case and do not be dissuaded from doing what you believe is right for the benefit of your child. It is very difficult to detach your feelings from what is objectively the best for your child. However if you don't do it, you may find the court doing it for you, and the outcome may not be what you desire.

23: Child Support: The Inside Track

Child support is an amount of money that non-resident parents pay regularly as a contribution towards the financial support for their children. Both parents have a legal responsibility to support their children financially if they can afford to do so.

If you cannot come to an amicable arrangement for child maintenance payments, the Child Support Agency (CSA) is likely to become involved.

The CSA exists to assess, collect and pay child support maintenance, ensuring that parents who live apart meet their financial obligations to their children. Its aim is to deliver an excellent child support service to help reduce child poverty and put children first by ensuring that absent parents are not allowed to shirk their responsibilities. The CSA has powers to order a parent to pay maintenance for a child.

The organisation is supposed to be the easiest and cheapest way to ensure that child maintenance is paid. However, those who use the service frequently complain of serious difficulties. There appears to be no uniformity of advice. Telephoning three different departments can result in three different answers to the same question.

Fees are set to be introduced for users of these services, and the CSA is set to be succeeded by a new organisation called the Child Maintenance Service (CMS). From 2014, every parent who requires its assistance will be charged a one-off fee of £20. An ongoing charge of between 7 per cent and 12 per cent is due to be levied on parents who rely on the CMS to collect child maintenance for them, and an ongoing charge of 15 per cent to 20 per cent will have to be paid by non-resident parents, on top of any child maintenance payments they make.

These proposed charges have prompted outrage in many quarters, with organisations such as Gingerbread, which campaigns on behalf of lone parents, pointing out that many parents turn to the CSA as a last resort, when all amicable methods to negotiate and collect child maintenance have failed. In other words, those will lose out are those who are least able to afford the new fees.

It is worth bearing in mind that originally, the proposed charges were significantly higher. They illustrate the Government's determination to push couples towards making private agreements, wherever possible, instead of relying upon publicly-funded organisations to make the arrangements. At its heart, this is nothing more than a cost-cutting exercise.

Private agreements

Parents can choose to opt out of the CSA by reaching agreement between themselves. Solicitors can assist. Private agreements save time – and from 2013, will save on fees too.

You can also ask your lawyer to pre-empt the CSA when preparing the financial settlement upon divorce, by combining spousal and child maintenance into one figure. This can then be enforced, even if an application to the CSA is later made by the other parent. This is called a Segal Order and means that even if the element assigned to child maintenance is reduced, the spousal maintenance increases pro-rata.

Please note, however, that a private agreement is not enforceable. If it fails, parties will have to apply to the CSA for an agreement calculation. This applies both to new cases, and to existing cases and arrangements.

Child Maintenance Options

Child Maintenance Options is part of the Department for Work and Pensions. It is a free and impartial information service, which helps parents make choices about child support.

I was recently invited to visit CMO, to see its team in action. There are 115 of them and, before being allowed to advise the general public, they undergo ten weeks' training. When I listened in on some of the calls and web chats, I was impressed. One caller, who lived with violence in the home, wanted information about launching a maintenance claim in difficult circumstances. I also sat in on a web chat with an angry father who refused to pay maintenance because he disagreed with the calculation.

All credit to Child Maintenance Options: although the team members aren't legal professionals, they deal with complex cases. They do all they can to help parents reach private agreements about child maintenance, without resorting to the overstretched CSA. A case will only be referred to the CSA when all other avenues have been exhausted. From what I saw, they provide considered responses to all the enquiries fired at them, without ever getting riled.

If you have any questions relating to child maintenance, I recommend that you contact CMO to see if they can help. You may be uncertain about the options available to you, for example. Or you may have a more specific question relating to, say, payment periods or absent parents.

If you wish to get in touch with CMO, you can find its contact details in the *Useful Resources* section of this book..

The CSA: starting blocks

The CSA is set to be folded into the CMS. However at the time of writing the timetable has yet to be confirmed. For clarity, I will continue to refer to the organisation as the "CSA".

1. **Unless you have a child maintenance agreement that predates 5 April 1993,** or a court order that predates April 2003, the CSA can help you.
2. **The CSA can act when the non-resident parent resides in the UK.** There are also reciprocal agreements with other child support agencies around the world, including Australia.
3. **Either party can apply to the CSA for a maintenance calculation,** except when there is a court order in place dated April 2003 onwards.
4. **When there is a court order in place that was made after April 2003,** the CSA is excluded for 12 months. After this time either parent can opt out of the order and apply for a CSA assessment.
5. **The CSA does not take student loans or other financial liabilities** of the non-resident parent into account when it calculates the sums of maintenance due.
6. **Following an initial calculation,** the CSA can take non-declared income and capital belonging to the non-resident parent into account. For example, if the parent owns a second property with equity of more than £65,000, a rental income will be attributed to this. Similarly if the parent is self employed or can control

their income, the CSA can attribute a higher income than has been officially declared to them.

7. **If the non-resident parent earns more than the CSA maximum** (currently £2,000 per week net income) you could be entitled to apply to the court for "top-up" payments. A court may well take the view that the non resident parent should make a greater contribution to the child's financial needs. The court also has the power to make orders relating to school fees. Let your solicitor advise you.

8. **The CSA has jurisdiction over the natural or adopted children of a relationship.** It does not deal with step-children or other "children of the family" following a relationship breakdown.

If you are a resident parent...

...Approaching the Child Support Agency can be a daunting prospect, but coping without money can be a lot worse. Making the other parent pay isn't an act of greed or retribution; it is simply asking them to contribute towards the upbringing of the children that they helped to bring into this world in the first place.

How the CSA reaches its figures

The CSA's calculations are based on the income of each party, with the assessment having a maximum ceiling of £104,000 take home pay per annum. If either party wishes to have income above this level taken into account, they may apply for additional maintenance through the courts.

Maintenance is calculated by the CSA according to a set

formula. The basic formula is that a parent who pays maintenance provides:

- **For one child:** 15 per cent of net income.
- **For two children:** 20 per cent of net income.
- **For three children:** 25 per cent of net income.

How much must non-resident parents pay?

Up until now, CSA maintenance has been calculated based
upon the net income of the non-resident parent. That is to
say, income after deductions of tax, national insurance, student loan repayments and pension contributions.

In December 2012, however, the Department of Work and
Pensions began rolling out a new formula: child maintenance,
calculated based upon the gross income of the non-resident
parents. That is to say, income before deductions of tax, national insurance, student loan repayments and pension contributions. Relevant information will be passed to the CMS by
HMRC.

The new formula is supposed to be simpler. At the time of
writing, it is being applied only when there are four or more
children in a family, and then only if the children have the
same two parents and the family has not had previous contact
with the CSA. For now, for smaller families, CSA maintenance
will continue to be calculated based upon net income. The
new formula is being rolled out extremely carefully and slowly: it will be applied to new cases first, with existing cases to be
transferred at a later date. It appears that having learned from
disastrous roll-outs in the past, the Government is reluctant
to apply the new formula to all cases until that formula has

DIVORCE & SPLITTING UP

been successfully tried and tested on a smaller group.

There are three bands of child support. For those on a weekly income of less than £100 per week, or who are on benefits, there is a £5 flat rate. Those with an income of £100 - £200 per week will pay the flat rate for the first £100 then a proportion of their income for the next £100.

The majority of claims will fall into the standard rate category, which covers any non-resident parent with a net income of between £200 and £2,000 per week. The formula is somewhat simplistic: 15% for one child; 20% for two children; 25% for three or more children.

There is provision for a reduced payment to be made if the non-resident parent is responsible for the children overnight more than 52 nights per year, on a sliding scale that starts at 1/7th discount of the weekly payment. Non-resident parents can also deduct a small amount of up to £15 per week for special expenses such as travel.

The CSA will also take into account any other child living with the non-resident parent for which they have financial responsibility.

If the non-resident parent pays child maintenance to more than one household, the total amount of maintenance will not exceed 25 per cent of the parent's net income and this amount is divided proportionately between the resident parents.

What if the non-resident parent earns more than £2,000 net per week?

The Children Act makes provision for special top-up payments to be awarded where the non-resident parent has an income above this level. This can take the form of increased maintenance level, paying for school fees, nursery fees and other extras.

As any top-up payment needs to be pursued through the courts, without support from the CSA, this effectively means there is a two tier system. A resident parent may need to apply to both the CSA and the court to obtain an appropriate level of maintenance.

Will I receive more maintenance because my child is disabled?

No. The CSA uses a flat rate calculator and does not factor in special educational or care needs. We have been asked if, in such circumstances, the court can order a top-up of mainte-nance. Unfortunately, this is not the case unless the non-res-ident parent has a net income in excess of £2,000 per week.

However, the resident parent can make an application through the courts in respect of provision of accommodation, capital and school fees where appropriate, regardless of the level of maintenance.

What if the non-resident parent won't pay?

The CSA has the power to deduct from the non-resident parent's wages at source to ensure payment. The agency also has the power to confiscate passports and driving licences as well as various enforcement and penal actions it has at its dis-posal.

The CSA has been heavily criticised for a lack of clout when it comes to self employed parents where income dries up, or when funds are diverted to a partner's or business account. Equally vocal have been the critics who point to the laborious process of appealing a CSA assessment felt to be too low to support the child's expected lifestyle.

Arrears are deducted as additional payments along with future child maintenance payments (in the same way that overpayments of benefits are deducted at source from future income and benefits).

In situations where there is a delay in the CSA making a ruling, or there is a prolonged investigation into the true financial picture, the payments will be backdated to the date of the application and arrears will be included into the monthly payments to be repaid over the next year.

In other words, for non-resident parents it's extremely important to respond promptly to CSA notifications and provides any information requested as soon as possible - you'll have to pay eventually.

What if I don't think I'm the father?

If your name is on a birth certificate, you were married to the mother at the time the child was born or if you refuse the offer of a DNA test, the CSA will assume you are the father. This is why it's extremely important to not ignore the agency's requests.

If the CSA contacts you about a child, but you do not believe you are the father you have the option to request a paternity test. The CSA requires that you pay for the DNA test in the first instance, but if the results of test show that you are not the father the CSA will reimburse the expense.

If a paternity test is taken at a later date, the parent must apply through the magistrates' or county courts for a declaration of non-parentage and obtain a paternity test from a specialist firm. Your solicitor will be able to assist with this somewhat complex procedure.

Note that the CSA does not refund child maintenance that has already been paid prior to contesting parentage.

If you resort to a DNA test, ensure that you have the test carried out by a recognised DNA laboratory such as CELL-MARK or the CSA may reject the test results as invalid. The CSA will not reimburse you for the costs of a declaration of non-parentage, nor the cost DNA test if this is not arranged through them.

What if I have to pay arrears and I can't afford them?

Payment of arrears is compulsory, but there is one course of action available to you. You can ring the CSA and apply to pay the arrears over a longer period of time. Note that this has to be agreed with them directly. Usually, they seek to recoup arrears within 12 months. However, if the arrears stretch across a period of time that is in excess of 12 months, you may wish to arrange to repay over 2 years or more.

When should I seek legal advice?

Liaising with the CSA can be a time consuming and fraught process, but your solicitor can communicate with them on your behalf. If you wish to contest an allegation of paternity, you solicitor can assist in arranging a DNA test and can advise you on your options following the results.

How can I appeal a CSA decision?

An appeal must be made within 1 month of the CSA's decision. If it is received outside of the time limit then the appeal may be disregarded. The CSA produces a leaflet detailing how to appeal and this includes an appeal application form. However, when considering an appeal, consider whether you are appealing the calculation or the timeframe over which this has to be paid. A risk of appeal is that the calculation may go up as well as down.

Upon receiving a valid appeal the CSA will contact you to try and resolve matters; if they are not resolved a submission is made by the CSA to the appeals tribunal. This includes all of the information that the CSA used to make their decision and all documents and information provided with the appeal application. This can be a long process and you are required to pay the assessed rate of child maintenance throughout.

A note on joint residency and child benefit

When there is a joint residency agreement in force, the parent in receipt of child benefits is deemed to be the resident parent and can apply for maintenance from the other parent. If a child's time is divided equally between both parents, the maintenance to be paid by the parent not in receipt of child benefits is calculated at the standard rate, but with a discount of 3/7ths. (This is the rate of discount when a child stays overnight with a non-resident parent for between 156 and 207 nights per annum.)

If there are two children, it may be that the parents agree to split the child benefits. If each parent is in receipt of benefits for one child then in theory, parents can make cross-applications - but in practice, most parents simply do not claim in these circumstances.

Dear Marilyn

I was devastated when I received the CSA assessment. My daughter's dad is successful and well off. He is a self-employed builder, and I know that he earns in the region of £55,000 per annum. I can only suppose that a lot of it is cash in hand, because his CSA assessment makes him out to be poverty-stricken! So they are saying that he only has to give our daughter £10 a week. It's a joke. What can I do to ensure that our daughter gets what she deserves?

Emma

Dear Emma,

If you think that his income is greater than that disclosed, you can apply to the CSA for a variation application. The CSA can look at his income again, using proof of additional income (such as work contracts) or by looking at his standard of living (such as the house he lives in, the cars he drives and holidays). The CSA does have a specialist team to deal with self-employed non-resident parents. Unfortunately variation is a long and difficult process. Incomes can be difficult to ascertain. If his income is largely cash or fluctuates, it may be that the CSA cannot prove to their satisfaction what his income is.

Marilyn

It isn't fashionable to say this, but I sympathise with the relatively untrained and inexperienced CSA staff who have to try and make sense of their work. As far as I am concerned, it is an impossible task for anybody other than trained family lawyers and family judges, because child maintenance is part of their everyday workload and is factored into the family's overall finances, rather than dealt with in isolation.

Back in the 1990s I was one of the first appointed Chairs of the Child Support Appeals Tribunal, hearing appeals against CSA assessments. I watched, horrified, as crooks who played the system and bamboozled CSA employees got away scot-free. Meanwhile naïve and trusting parents and children, desperate for money, were ignored. Where did the justice go? I had no judicial discretion and I could not, in all conscience, be part of a purely administrative system of law. So, I resigned.

Since then I have watched from the sidelines as - predictably - the system has tumbled into ruins. Millions of devastated people have been left behind in its wake, and billions of taxpayers' money has been spent.

Since then, various reforms have attempted to do away with all the old failings, with limited success. Even so, you should seek to familiarise yourself with the changes that are being planned; before you know it, they could be brought to bear on your own family arrangements.

Coming up: the eight most important changes to child maintenance

The latest set of reforms to child maintenance aim to simplify and streamline assessments, and improve the collection process. The most significant changes, all of which are due to come into force between now and the end of 2014, are as follows:

1. **It will no longer be compulsory** for a parent on benefits to apply to the CSA.

2. **A parent in receipt of benefits** will be able to retain a greater amount of the child maintenance paid through the CSA: £20 per week instead of £10.

3. **Money parents receive in child maintenance payments** is not taken into account when calculating that parent's out-of-work benefits or Housing and Council Tax benefits.

4. **Gross income rather than net income** will be used to determine CSA liability (see above).

5. **The flat rate of maintenance will increase** for those earning less than £200 net per week, from £5 per week to £7.

6. **Powers of enforcement are set to increase.** These include deducting child maintenance directly from the non-resident parent's bank accounts, and confiscating passports, curfews and powers to negotiate repayment, or to reclaim payment from the estate of a deceased parent.

7. **A change to enforcement will mean that in many cases,** the Department of Work and Pensions will no longer need to apply to the court to take enforcement action against a non-resident parent who refuses to pay. The new procedure will be more streamlined, and purely administrative.

8. **Maintenance calculations will be fixed for one**

year and then reviewed. Calculations will not be reviewed earlier unless income fluctuates by more than 25 per cent. This measure aims to give both parents more financial security.

At the time of writing, the details of many of these proposed changes have yet to be clarified. If in doubt you can visit my blog, www.marilynstowe.co.uk, for regular updates on child maintenance matters.

24: What's the Deal with Dad?

Dear Marilyn

Please tell me something. I love my children and every day of their lives, I have been involved in bringing them up. So why is it that now I am divorced from their mother, my involvement has been relegated to once or twice a week, at defined hours? It's distressing for me and it's distressing for my children. Do you have any idea how bad I feel? Or how terrible it is for my children, who are used to having me around 24/7? Effectively I am no longer parenting. Instead, I am a visitor.

Andrew

Dear Andrew,

First of all, thank you for sharing your perspective. It is fair to say that until relatively recently, courts and lawyers hadn't appreciated the father's viewpoint as much as they might have. Fortunately this has changed and continues to change.

So what to do? Shared residence orders are no longer uncommon. In fact they are encouraged because they allow both parents to continue parenting. Go and see a solicitor who specialises in children matters and discuss this possibility with them. Providing that your proposals are practical and

*put the children's welfare first, they may well suc-
ceed. It does not matter if you were not married to
the children's mother.*

*Such an order can be expensive to obtain: each
side pays their own costs. At least (or should that
be "at last"?) courts are beginning to recognise that
children should be encouraged to spend time with
their fathers as well as their mothers.*

Marilyn

Parents suffer when they lose the precious experience of
living with their children on a day-to-day basis. I have lost
count of the number of times a parent has come to see me in
tears because they no longer see their child every day. Sadly,
the inevitable consequence of living in two households is that
even if there is an equal division of time, one parent is bound
to miss out on something.

At one time it was almost automatic that in the event of divorce, children went to live with their mother. Judges, social
workers and society at large presumed this was the "natural"
way of things. There is little doubt that the position for fathers today is much better than a decade ago. Much of that is
down to the changes that have taken place in society and how
the roles and rights of men and women have developed. For
instance, it is no longer unusual for the wife to be the breadwinner while the man stays at home to care for the children.

Even so, many of today's men feel that they are second
class citizens when it comes to residency of the children or
contact arrangements with them. In too many divorces, chil-

dren become weapons: the means by which emotional blows can be landed. A few years ago it was estimated that up to 50 per cent of all fathers lost touch with their children within a couple of years of a divorce. That is a shocking statistic.

In my experience, if a man puts together a cogent and reasoned argument about why he should have residency of his children, the courts are prepared to look at his argument in an even-handed way. However groups campaigning for fathers' rights say that they have experienced markedly different fates at the judges' hands. These angry men feel wronged by the courts, and cruelly torn from their children.

I have dealt with every type of relationship breakdown. I represent equal numbers of men and women and because I work to achieve for my clients the satisfactory conclusion that they seek, I have been sheltered from the kind of resentment and sense of injustice that the men who join these organisations clearly feel.

However, I have much sympathy for their cause. After speaking to a number of these men and being moved by their stories, I could only conclude that many fathers are unfairly treated by the law in this country. Many of the men to whom I spoke told me that that they had taken active, sharing roles as parents, only to find themselves suddenly expunged from the daily lives of their children.

My advice to men who find themselves in this situation, or who fear that they will end up in this situation, is as follows:

    1. Stay calm. Focus on what your children are telling you that they want. You may not agree with their views, but you need to recognise that the court will look at your family situation from the children's perspective. Your case will be harmed if you disregard the children's wishes and feelings.

2. **Acquaint yourself with CAFCASS:** the court-appointed welfare officers (www.cafcass.gov.uk). Somebody from CAFCASS will meet all the family members and determine how everybody feels about the situation. They will take into account the children's wishes and feelings, and will report back to the court with their recommendations.

3. **Parental Alienation Syndrome is a term used to describe a parent's poisoning of a child's mind against the other parent.** It is a controversial concept, and not all courts in the UK accept that the syndrome exists. However the court will recognise when a child shows a disproportionate reaction to one parent, and will seek to get to the bottom of why this is the case.

4. **Family courts have received a drubbing over the years because until recently, they made their decisions behind closed doors.** If you are required to attend a family court, remember they are not "out to get you". Whatever you do, do not rant or rail against them because you won't improve their opinion of you if you come across as unreasonable or aggressive.

5. **Don't wage war against "The Man".** It is possible that at some point, somebody in authority will say something with which you do not agree. However this does not mean that you should complain about them or try to get them removed from the case. As difficult as

it is, recognise that there may be a reason behind a rec-
ommendation. For example, if you have not seen your
children for a long time, the court may recommend that
contact is supervised until the children's trust in you
has been rebuilt.

6. **Brave the contact centres.** Yes, they can be intim-
idating or unpleasant places. However if your contact
with your children is reduced to a few hours at one of
these centres, with or without supervision, grit your
teeth and look towards the future. Remember: you are
there for your children and the contact centre is merely
a stepping stone towards a full and renewed role in your
children's lives.

When one parent does not co-operate

What happens when a court orders contact for a non-resident parent, but one of the parties does not abide by that
order? All contact orders have a warning notice on them, to
warn parents of the consequences of non-compliance. In the
past, the court's enforcement powers have included the following measures:

- Committing a parent to prison or making a suspended
  imprisonment order, which may not achieve the rein-
  statement of contact.
- Imposing a fine, which may deprive a parent on a limited
  budget and may not be consistent with the welfare of the
  child;
- Transferring residence, although this may not be a suitable option if the other parent does not have the capacity

to care for the child full-time.

• Directing a parent to participate in an activity that would promote contact with a child, or making it a condition of a contact order that the parent undertakes such an activity. Contact activities could include parenting classes or counselling sessions that assist a parent to establish, maintain or improve contact.

• Imposing a community-based enforcement order (see below), requiring the parent to do unpaid work. The type of work is determined by a probation officer.

• Ordering one parent to pay the other compensation for financial loss resulting from the breach of an order. This could include, for example, the cost of a pre-arranged holiday or outing if one parent had prevented the child from going at the last moment, without reasonable excuse.

• CAFCASS officers can monitor compliance with a contact order, activities and enforcement, and report back to the court.

Enforcement orders

When a court is satisfied beyond reasonable doubt that a parent has failed to comply with a contact order, it has the power to make an enforcement order. This requires the parent to undertake up to 200 hours' unpaid work. The provisions are similar to the community orders in the criminal courts.

The court may not make an order if the person had a reasonable excuse for failing to comply. An enforcement order can be suspended, depending on the circumstances, and more than one enforcement order can be made by the court. The person in breach of the contact order must have first been informed about or given a copy of the contact order's warning notice.

To apply for an enforcement order, you must either be the person with whom the child lives, the person whose contact is provided for in the order, an individual *"subject to a condition or contact activity imposed by the court order"*, or, with leave from the court, the child named in the contact order.

Before making an enforcement order the court must:

1. Be satisfied that an enforcement order is necessary to ensure compliance and that the likely effect on the person is proportionate to the breach of the contact order.
2. Obtain and consider information about the person, including information about their religious beliefs and work commitments, and the likely effect of the enforcement order on them.
3. Take the child's welfare into account.

The Court must ask a CAFCASS officer to monitor or arrange for the monitoring of the person's compliance with the unpaid work requirement and to report to the Court. The current arrangement is for the National Offender Management Services (NOMS) to be responsible for arranging the unpaid work. The supervisor will be an officer employed by the National Probation Service, who will report to CAFCASS.

An alternative to an enforcement order

If a contact order has been breached and an enforcement order is not suitable, the court can order the person in breach to pay compensation to another person who has suffered financial loss as a result of that breach. The application must be made by the person who has suffered the financial loss. The court must take into account the individual's financial circumstances when determining the level of any compensation, but the sum may not exceed the applicant's loss. The compensation ordered to be paid is a civil debt.

Do note, however, that if a reasonable excuse for the breach is presented to the court, compensation may not be ordered.

25: Helping Your Children Through Divorce

The number of children affected by divorce represents a disturbing legacy for society, not least because we hope these children will be able to form stable, long-term relationships of their own in the future. They will have seen their parents fight, scream and cry. They will feel upset and uncertain about what the future holds, and often they will feel torn in their loyalty to both parents.

Children are sharp and sensitive to their surroundings. Even if Mum and Dad save the crockery-throwing and accusations of intolerable behaviour for those times when the kids are out of the house, a child is soon going to realise that all is not well. So what you do to put the children first and minimise the pain they feel?

How to prepare children for divorce

Telling your children that the family is breaking up will be one of the hardest things that you ever do. Whatever you do, make it very clear that you both love the children, that it is not their fault the relationship is over and that they are not "leaving" either parent. For further help, see chapter 10.

Here are some other dos and don'ts:

Don't involve the children in any rows. They may already feel that it is somehow their fault; being dragged into the middle of it all will only intensify their feelings of guilt.

Do give constant reassurance to your children that they are not to blame, that they are still loved by both parents and, whatever may happen in the future, that this will always be the case.

Don't put any pressure upon your children to take sides. To subject them to this would be bordering on abuse. A child with torn loyalties to parents can grow up scarred and confused.

Do present a united front with the other parent in all discussions and decisions involving the children – even when this means that you must do this through gritted teeth. It is extremely distressing and disturbing for a child to discover that his parents are arguing over his future.

Don't put pressure on younger children to make decisions about their own care. By all means take their feelings into account, but don't expect them to choose.

Do encourage your children to express their opinions and feelings. Some children feel unable to do so, through fear of alienating one or other parent. But seething resentment and bottled-up unhappiness will keep them from moving on.

Don't give into the temptation to pour your soul out to your children. Children are desperate for their parents' good opinion and will often tell you what you want to hear, which will only compound their feelings of discomfort and guilt.

Do remember that divorce is just as frightening and bewildering for the children as it is for you. So keep them up-to-date with events and be honest with them, short of burdening them with the ugly details.

Don't tell your children about the other parent's misde-
meanours. Just tell them that Mummy and Daddy
are no longer happy living together. Children are
usually tempted to try to push their parents back
together. This rarely works out, and it's easier for
them to come to terms with their family breakdown if they have some idea of the reason behind
it.

Do set boundaries. Successful boundaries, along with
respect for the other parties, will benefit everyone.
Don't interfere when your former partner has care
of the children and don't permit your former partner to encroach on your space. Redefine your relationship to ensure that each of you respects the
other's choices and personal parenting styles –
even if they differ.

It takes two to tango

Parents can lose sight of their long-term objectives if they
get bogged down in day-to-day emotions, particularly if they
are faced with a situation that they feel they must "win" at all
costs. When parents cannot agree and the matters end up in
court, judges tend to be very critical of a parent who is con-
trolling, aggressive or unreasonable when the other has simply asked for respect and personal space.

If you are doing your best for your children but your former partner appears to have his or her priorities in a different
order, it isn't easy. Just do your best to be the bigger person
and to choke down what may be a very natural sense of rage or
injustice. In the long-term it is for the good of your children.

Dear Marilyn

My husband left me last year, after meeting another woman at work. We have two sons aged five and eight. I do try to put a brave face on things but the children are bewildered and hurt. They don't know why their daddy has gone and although he makes the effort to see them at weekends, it isn't the same.

Last weekend, after he brought the children back, they were telling me all about the nice lady they had met. I realised they had been introduced to my husband's girlfriend. I was horrified! I feel it is far too soon for my sons to meet this woman, and I am furious that I was not consulted beforehand.

His behaviour shows a complete lack of regard for our family. I am beginning to think that I have been too nice and let him get away with far too much, for far too long. What should I do?

Bridget

Dear Bridget,

If this woman's relationship with your husband is likely to endure, the children will have to meet her at some stage. The only questions are: when and how? It isn't easy or pleasant for you, but the hard truth is this: if the children get to know her with your blessing, they will adapt to their new situation *far more easily.*

Introductions to new partners must be sensitively handled. In this case, your partner has taken the decision and the preparations out of your hands. Such behaviour does not commend itself, but what's done is done. In truth, I have never known a mother to be happy when her children are introduced to a new woman.

Children absorb their parents' emotions. They absorb bitterness, anger and distress, and can express these feelings in distressing ways. The best parents are those who can look beyond their own hurt. They manage to put their grievances to one side and accept that their children enjoy spending time with both parents. Children do love their parents - usually in spite of their actions rather than because of them.

Marilyn

How to help children to move on

Your children will need time to adjust to their new situation; the issuing of the decree absolute may not provide the sense of closure for them that it will to you. In the weeks, months and years following your divorce, there will be a number of flashpoints involving you, your former partner and your children. These are situations and "firsts" that must be navigated with care and sensitivity. Begin thinking about them now, and you can prepare for them in good time.

Parents' Evening: as parents you both have the same responsibilities to your child. In an ideal world you would be able to attend parent's evening together. Failing that, make appointments to speak to the teachers separately. If there are any problems at school you must discuss these with the other parent. After all your child's needs are of paramount importance.

Mother's Day and Father's Day: the usual rule of thumb is that the child spends Mother's Day with their mother and Father's Day with their father, regardless of the usual arrangement. If this cannot be agreed then the court can be asked to decide. But be warned: the court will not be impressed by your failure to agree such a minor matter.

Child's Birthday: another important day in a child's life. Ideally, parents would arrange birthday parties jointly and would both spend some time with the child on his or her birthday. Alternatively parents can arrange parties on alternate years, or alternate the birthday morning and birthday evening between parents.

School Plays and Sports Day: you both have an equal right to attend these important events in your child's life. If joint attendance will lead to arguments, however, think carefully before subjecting your child to additional conflict. As before, if you can agree and at least be civil to one another, this is best for your children. Conflict inevitably arises when a new partner attends the child's play with one parent, and the other parent is left seething in the audience. Don't make this harder than it needs to be. If the play runs for more than one night, think about going on different days.

Summer Holidays: courts are increasingly inclined towards an equal division of school holidays, but do consider your work commitments before you seek additional contact during this period. Try to be considerate of the other parent's needs and arrangements. If your children are very young, think carefully before whisking them off to hot places or on long journeys just because you can. Above all, remember this is your child's holiday! Make sure they enjoy it and don't begrudge them a day with their other parent if the alternative is a summer club or a babysitter.

Christmas: the majority of families operate on an alternate year arrangement, but this does not suit everyone. If you are happy to swap Christmas Day and Boxing Day between you, then fine. Alternatively you can split the day in two. Don't forget that the day is for your child and don't allow them to feel torn between their parents. Under no circumstances feed them up just because you know the other parent is having a big meal later in the day. The only person who will suffer will be the child, who will eat too much trying to please you both.

Meeting a parent's new partner for the first time: this is a tricky one and should be treated with tact on both sides. Avoid criticism of your ex's new partner, regardless of your feelings towards them. If you are the one doing the introducing, no child should be made to feel they have been replaced. Avoid comparisons with the child's other parent at all costs and don't introduce your new partner as a "new mum" or "new dad", because the child will simply be confused and frightened by the changes implied.

Remarrying: it happens! As people move on with their lives, they form new relationships. If and when this happens, reassure the child that they still have a role in your life and that you love them. Involve them in the ceremony and make it special for them too. If your former partner is remarrying, rise above it. Put your child first and be civil. Don't threaten to prevent your child going to the wedding as you will be the ogre in the story. Above all remember that children find weddings exciting - and that you too may want the same courtesy at some point in the future.

CASEBOOK

Mr I and his former wife were so wrapped up in their personal disputes, they forgot to put their children first.

This couple had eight-year-old twins, who thought the world of both their parents. The couple had parted ways because Mr I had met someone else and moved out of the family home. Both parents loved their children dearly and were more than capable of providing for them. However Mr I's former wife had never forgiven him for leaving, had railed in court about his inadequacies as a father and had long maintained that Mr I's girlfriend was an unsuitable role model for her children.

When Mr I announced that he was marrying his girlfriend, he asked his twins to be bridesmaid and page boy. The children were over the moon. Then their mother discovered that the wedding was not set for a day on which Mr I had contact. She used this opportunity to insist that she should have the twins at Christmas (this being the father's year). Mr I was distraught. He had been put in the difficult position of having to choose between his wedding and Christmas. He felt that he was being blackmailed. Meanwhile his former wife believed that she was being asked to give up more and more time with the children without any recompense or thought for her.

One of the lawyers from our children's department was in an unenviable position. She had to go to court to tell a judge that these parents could not even agree over two days in a year. Two days that were set to rank amongst the most exciting and happy days in the children's lives.

The judge was scathing in his response. The matter took several hours to be settled, with both parents under pressure from the court to reach a compromise for their children's interests. To the relief of all, the situation was eventually resolved. The twins were able to enjoy both their father's wedding and their family's Christmas.

26: Grandparents, Stepfamilies and Contact Orders

Dear Marilyn

Our son was divorced from his wife three years ago. They have two beautiful children, and we have done our best to keep in touch. We babysat regularly, until the children's mother moved 150 miles away. Recently we called our former daughter-in-law to try and arrange a visit. She declined, telling us she was engaged to somebody new and had decided that her family should "break off the ties" with their old life. We don't want to create a fuss as we don't want to cause our grandchildren further distress. But we miss then terribly. What would you recommend we do?

Hazel

Dear Hazel,

You are in a difficult situation. You don't want to upset your grandchildren, but at the same time there is a risk that they will blame you for their alienation. Reach out to them. Write to them, send cards and presents for birthdays and Christmas, and invite them to stay with you. Make it clear to your daughter-in-law that you aren't trying to interfere with her life but simply want to keep in

> *touch with your grandchildren. You can consider an application to court if necessary, but you should also know that an application will inevitably draw battle lines between your daughter-in-law and yourselves. Do the children see your son? If so, perhaps you can arrange to share some of that time with them?*
>
> *Marilyn*

The breakdown of your relationship will affect people outside the household, as well as those within it. The impact upon grandparents and other family members can be profound. They may be left with feelings of grief and loss, particularly if they are relatives of the partner who no longer lives with the children. The time that the children spend with them is likely to be reduced, at best.

Divorce can be difficult for grandparents, even if they never liked their child's spouse. Not only must they watch as their son's or daughter's life is torn apart but, in the case of the paternal grandparents, they must to face up to the very real possibility that they may never see their grandchildren again. Unless a strong bond has been built up between a mother and her former parents-in-law, paternal grandparents may lose touch. In other cases, visitors are only grudgingly allowed as a kind of trade-off for maintenance payments. If a resident parent is struggling to maintain good relations with their former partner, the need to maintain regular contact with the former partner's parents may become an additional and unwanted burden.

There are other cases, of course, where the lack of contact results from sheer bloody-mindedness on the part of the resident parent. Having been hurt by the divorce, he or she takes revenge by obstructing the grandparents' access at every possible opportunity, often to the detriment of the children's happiness.

Members of stepfamilies may feel the same concerns and emotions. Step-parents and step-siblings may have spent years living with the children in the family home, forging strong relationships. If these relationships are snatched away, or those bonds are broken, the resulting unhappiness and turmoil will affect both households.

Dear Marilyn

My son has stopped me seeing my twin grandsons, aged three, and I am finding this very hard to cope with. I have had contact with the children since they were born, but eight months ago my son decided not to talk to me at all and said that I must not visit. This has made life unbearable as I love our grandchildren dearly.

I promise you that I have been a loving parent and grandparent, but my son has had issues with me because I have never got on with his partner. She hasn't spoken to me for nearly two years. My letters to my son have been ignored.

Pat

Dear Pat,

It is very sad that the relationship between you and your son has broken down. It is, I think, a resumption of that relationship which is the key to seeing your grandchildren again. However your letters touches only in passing on what I believe is the main issue causing problems: namely, your relationship with your son's partner. You don't give any reasons for your son's decisions but surely he must have communicated something to you when you were seeing your grandchildren?

Were you critical of his partner without realising it? Are you overly critical of her? Is she resentful, angry, hurt, upset? Does she think that you do not make an effort to build bridges with her? Are any apologies due? Do you show plenty of love and affection towards your grandchildren, but none to your son and his partner? I am not saying that you are to blame, but if this situation is going to improve I think you need to do some soul-searching as to why the relationship between you and your grandchildren's parents has broken down so catastrophically.

Going forward, is there anyone trusted by all of you who could become an intermediary, to try and resolve this situation? If not, are you all prepared to try family therapy, or mediation - or even go to court? Going to court doesn't mean that you will end up with a contested court hearing. There are

opportunities to settle along the way. If your son and his partner refused to budge, you could always withdraw your application to avoid that final confrontation. If you do go to court there is no guarantee of a successful outcome, but you are unlikely to end up with a costs bill against you unless there are very serious reasons why the application should never have been made. The general rule in children cases is that there is no order for costs.

The alternative is to leave this situation alone and wait for time to pass. Your son and his partner may yet come round.

Regards,

Marilyn

Dear Marilyn

My second marriage ended last year. I have a son from my first marriage; my former wife has a son of a similar age, and the two boys became inseparable. My biological son moved out of the family home with me; however, he is finding it difficult to cope without his stepbrother, who is his best friend in the world. We have moved to a different town, so the boys no longer see one another at school; for reasons best known to her, my former wife is pouring cold water on my efforts to arrange *regular meet-ups for the boys. They are aged nine and ten.*

What would you recommend in these circumstances?

Anthony

Dear Anthony,

You can make an application to the court to have contact with your former wife's child. The court will be interested in the welfare of both children and given what you describe, I expect they will soon be back in touch.

Marilyn

How to apply for a contact order

If you are a grandparent or another extended family member, what legal action can you take in situations such as these? In the past, contact orders were occasionally granted to grandparents - but only rarely. Today, they are increasingly common as the court recognises the role of extended family and how important it is for a child to know his or her family background.

Again, it is always preferable for the parties to resolve the issues themselves. Nothing, of course, prevents extended family from seeing the children during parental contact.

If they cannot, it is worth remembering that the court considers it best for children to know their extended family, so that they can understand their background and place in the world.

Anyone can apply to a court for contact with a child, but there would need to be unusual circumstances for a grandparent to make a sole application. The court will first consider the need for parental contact; after that has been factored in, is there any time left? Nothing, of course, prevents extended family members from seeing the children during parental contact.

If you wish to apply for contact with a grandchild, you must first apply to the court for "leave" to be heard. As the grandparent or step-parent you do not have parental responsibility, so you are not automatically entitled to make a court application in relation to a child. The court will consider the family circumstances and the role that the person seeking leave has within that family. For example, the court will distinguish between a grandparent who frequently assists with childcare and a grandparent who lives out of the country and sees their grandchild once every few years.

Once leave is obtained, the court will consider the practicalities. It will take into account the children's wishes and feelings, as well as the children's established routine. A court will prefer to make provision for the children to see grandparents within existing contact arrangements if possible, rather than carve the children's time into smaller portions. The court will also consider whether an order is needed or whether matters can be agreed. The court will normally instruct CAFCASS to become involved. CAFCASS is able to interview all parties and speak to the children. Its role is to investigate, assist in discussions and report to the judge with recommendations.

A grandparent cannot obtain Parental Responsibility unless a residence order is made in their favour. This means that a grandparent or step-parent does not have any legal entitlement to any say in schooling or medical treatment for example. Unless the children already live with you, the court is unlikely to make a residence order or a shared residence order save for circumstances where one or both of the parents are dead or deemed unsuitable to care for the children.

Advice for grandparents

- Try to discuss matters with the child's parents at an early stage. Make it clear that you are not taking sides and that you simply want an ongoing role in your grandchild's life. Don't play the blame game or get involved in the relationship breakdown.
- If discussions do not proceed smoothly or if you have concerns for your grandchildren, don't let the situation escalate. Instead, seek legal advice.
- Be realistic. If the grandchildren are only seeing your son or daughter once a fortnight, it is unlikely that you will see them as frequently as you may have done previously. Don't forget that the children now have three households to move between - not just yours and theirs.
- Consider whether your application should be linked to your son's or daughter's application for contact. The court is more willing to consider an application by a grandparent to assist with childcare within the context of the parents being primary carers, particularly if historically, you have been the babysitter of choice.
- Don't use an application as a way of getting back at your

son or daughter-in-law. Don't use your application as a way to reduce their time with their children and don't use it as a weapon. The court will be highly critical of any person who appears to be abusing the process or using the law as a means to hurt the other parties.

- Do try to discuss matters both with your grandchildren and their parents. If you apply for contact, ensure that the contact you are applying for is what they want. Your grandson isn't going to be your greatest fan if he has to miss his football training every Saturday morning so that you can visit.

- If parents can resolve the issues themselves, it is more likely that grandparents' hopes and wishes will be considered.

- You don't have to wait for the divorce to go through before you apply for an order.

- A contact order can take the form of meetings, letters, cards or telephone calls. In some cases, courts prefer to establish a pattern of contact slowly, working up from letters to face-to-face time. This can be the case if there has previously been limited contact, or the child lives a long way away.

CASEBOOK

Mrs P came to see me for the first time, accompanied by her mother. The client was well-groomed and smartly-dressed. Her mother, meanwhile, looked drawn and tired. Mrs P asked if I would mind if she removed her wig. I hadn't realised she was wearing one. She sat through the interview, completely bald, and told me about her cancer. She had a life expectancy of about 20 months at most, and she had come to discuss her children's future. She was 38 and had two children, aged eight and six.

When he had learned about her cancer, her husband had left her. He had been unable to face her illness, and for many months had been having an affair. He had told her that she could have whatever she wanted from him and that his affair "wasn't serious". Mrs P's concern was for the children: she wanted her mother to care for them following her death.

I gave her advice that I hoped helped her. I told her not to give up, to fight for her life and let me look after the legal side. I informed her about the divorce process and the availability of expedited hearings, which would speed up the proceedings. I emphasised the importance of making a will, and severing the joint tenancy in relation to her home, so that it did not automatically pass to her husband. I explained that if she set up a trust fund with her estate, to be held for the benefit of the children, she could appoint independent, professional trustees to administer it.

The most difficult question to tackle was who

would care for the children after their parent's death. Neither Mrs P nor her mother, who clearly loathed the husband, wished him to play any major part in the children's future. The grandmother told me how she planned to take the children to live with her. However, I had to advise her that their father was likely to be awarded the children's care. I felt it would be better to try and agree beforehand what would happen as I assumed the children would wish to remain in their home - of which the father already owned half. He could - and no doubt would - expect the children to live with him because of their age. However difficult, they had to pull together in one direction for the benefit of the children, who would need all their relatives when the time came.

Grandparents will always play a supportive role, but often their age is against them. Mrs P and her mother reluctantly agreed. There is no perfect answer in a case as tragic as this one.

Part VII: What Could Go Wrong?

27: Top Ten Dirty Divorce Tricks

For certain people, divorce brings their very worst qualities to the fore.

Divorce is an emotional rollercoaster. When people are really hurting, particularly if they have been "swapped" for somebody else, self-preservation becomes all-important. For some, such a state of mind leads to all-consuming hatred, malice and a desire for vengeance.

As I said at the beginning of this book: after 30 years as a divorce solicitor, nothing surprises me anymore. Here is my countdown of the top ten dirty divorce tricks. I wish to stress that none of them are recommended. Indeed, some of them are illegal!

1. **Moving the spouse to a different country, in order to obtain a more favourable divorce settlement.** This may sound far-fetched but, as I have noted in chapter 15, this happens more frequently than one might think. The trusting spouse does not realise that the promised life of sun and fun is never destined to materialise. Instead, a divorce looms in a country in which financial settlements are far more modest than in rainy England.

2. **If your spouse encourages a move abroad, make sure that you agree beforehand what will happen if your relationship falters.** Before leav-

ing the country, consider entering into a postnuptial agreement (like a prenuptial agreement, but one that takes place after the wedding), which regulates where a divorce would take place, where the children would live and how a financial settlement would be worked out.

3. **Covert surveillance of a spouse by bugging the phone, the car, the office** - or by employing an enquiry agent. When a spouse is suspected of having an affair, all sorts of surveillance techniques can be used. One client told me that her husband would wait until he was in the car to discuss his affair with friends, or with the Other Woman herself. The wife placed a recorder beneath the car seat, and recorded all his telephone calls. Although it gave her satisfaction, I questioned the need in law. It isn't necessary for a divorce, and is likely to leave the judge wondering about the character of someone who goes to these lengths. When discretion is needed for a financial settlement, this type of conduct can backfire.

4. **Secretly photocopying every scrap of financial information in the house and office.** Also: downloading everything from a spouse's computer, and later pretending that he/she didn't realise what he/she was doing. What often happens is that a piece of computer equipment is purchased with which to download the computer's hard drive. Or an IT expert is surreptitiously called in. Either way, the spouse obtains information illegally, and risks penalties ranging from a fine to prosecution. Don't go there.

5. **Salting away as much money as possible,** ready

for that "rainy day". Many clients know that they are going to get divorced long before proceedings are set in motion. They decide to take pre-emptive action and hide their money. Wealthy people do this by shipping it offshore into untraceable bank accounts, owned via a warren of trusts and companies. The less well off do it by depositing funds into the bank accounts of relatives. The most extreme case I have come across was that of a spouse who had placed more or less everything the couple had into an untouchable offshore trust. He then began to borrow against all the rest of the non-trust assets onshore. Fortunately his wife became wise to his ploy. She was able to injunct him and put a stop to it. In other cases, companies are sold and the monies "squatted" long before the divorce takes place, or afterwards when it is too late to do anything more about it.

6. **Damage, destruction or sale of the household's most valuable contents - particularly those the spouse wishes to keep.** Lady Graham Moon has gone down in English family law history for acting like a milkman, except that she was delivering to her neighbours the contents of her estranged husband's valuable wine cellar. Cases I have personally encountered include:

- A wife who sold the Steinway piano without the knowledge of her pianist husband.
- A wife who sawed the legs off a Chippendale cabinet and delivered it - along with its removed legs - to her husband.

- A wife who ran a bath of scalding water and bleach, into which she dumped all her husbands' suits and ties.
- Some clients claim to have sold assets at for remarkably low prices; miraculously, these same assets reappear in their ownership once the case is over. I have known this to happen with valuable jewellery, art - and even an aeroplane!

7. **Spending money wildly, as a form of "payback".** Some spurned wives choose to take revenge by spending as much as they can on their husbands' credit cards before the husbands realise what is going on. One client of mine with an Amex Centurion card received a credit card bill for £30,000 for jewellery purchased by his wife from Cartier. A further £20,000 had been taken off his card, to pay her lawyer's bills. In such cases, household bills may well be left unpaid. The court does have power to add back wasted monies, so all is not lost.

8. **Assaulting the spouse and the new partner.** This tends to prove much more satisfying if it takes place in public, thus causing the maximum possible embarrassment. I was involved with one case in which the wife was found to have hired a hitman against her husband. In another case, the wife threw a brick through the front window of her dentist husband's surgery. This was a whammy in more ways than one as the glass shattered all over the practice nurse - also the husband's new lover - who had been sitting at her desk by the window!

9. **Using a friend as a spy, to gain access to the lawyer's office and learn at firsthand what is going on.** This is the height of sneakiness. A girlfriend pre-

tends to befriend the wife, offers a helping hand with the lawyers, gets to know the tactics and advice - and then reports everything back to the husband.

10. **"Conflicting out" the spouse's lawyer.** A good lawyer can bring about an extremely successful outcome. It is better to get that lawyer onside, or make sure that the lawyer is placed out of bounds. Many times I have been aware that this is happening to me. On one occasion, the husband telephoned ahead for an emergency appointment and was prepared to fly over from the Caribbean to see me. On another occasion, a husband thought he had successfully conflicted me out.... by consulting a lawyer at my husband's offices. Sadly for him our two firms, Stowe Family Law LLP and Grahame Stowe Bateson, are completely separate. His dirty trick failed.

11. **If all else fails...running off with the divorce lawyer!** Truth is sometimes stranger than fiction, and this has been known to happen. It certainly gives an unfair advantage, with vastly reduced legal fees. In one case, a devious spouse began an affair with his divorce lawyer. Having paid out his wife, he swiftly married his well-to-do new love!

28: How to Act in Court: Dos and Don'ts

Clients don't always realise that how they dress, act and speak can be crucial factors that may weigh on a judge's mind during a case. When there is a decision to be made in favour of the client, or against them, the smallest details can make a difference.

For this reason, it is extremely important that you have some idea of how you are expected to behave. Time and time again I am taken aback by the naivety of both men and women whose conduct in court is nothing short of idiocy. From the man who wears a thousand-pound suit and brash Rolex, only to claim he is impoverished, to the attention-seeking wife who displays more than her emotions to the court, this kind of conduct could undermine the entire legal argument. I cannot invent a case, but I can advise on subtle detail, so here are some tips for you:

1. **Always dress in a sombre and modest way.** Men should refrain from loud check jackets and flashy watches. Women: avoid multi coloured diamond studded nail varnish and see through tops.
2. **Tell the truth. Don't be tempted to tell even a little lie.** You will be found out and could lose the sympathy of the court.
3. **Even when the pressure is reaching fever pitch**, always behave respectfully and calmly.
4. **Don't lose your temper** or you will lose your case.
5. **If you break down and cry, that is not uncommon.** Don't allow yourself to feel like a fool. You aren't.

6. **Take your time answering questions.** Speak clearly.

7. **If you know the answer, give it.** You aren't on trial. The court is simply deciding how to sort out the assets.

8. **If you don't know the answer**, say so.

9. **Don't ever guess.** If you have made a mistake, admit it. The judge is assessing your evidence and will give you credit for telling the truth, even if it isn't easy. Remember that the judge has many years of experience; if you try and paint a wholly angelic picture of yourself, the judge will find this hard to believe.

10. **Don't ever think that if a load of nonsense sounds good to you,** it will to the judge.

11. **When your spouse is giving evidence, keep calm.** Don't shout out. If you wish to, make notes and hand them to your lawyer. But don't distract your lawyer unless it is vital.

13. **Don't make the mistake of maligning your spouse.** Don't keep harping on about his or her vices and failings. No-one wants to hear this, and you could risk losing the court's sympathy.

14. **Don't tip a jug of water over your opponent's head, as Heather Mills did.** While it will make you feel better, it may also land you in the cells.

29: Other Pitfalls, and How to Avoid Them

Illegal snooping

In matrimonial proceedings, both parties have an obligation of full and frank disclosure of their financial position to the court. Sometimes parties think a spouse will not make such disclosure and decide to collect evidence they believe will not otherwise be produced. I think this happens frequently, but solicitors must advise clients to behave within the law at all times, irrespective of a spouse's behaviour.

It is not permitted to intercept and open post before it has been delivered to the correct address. Documents obtained by such means must be returned and cannot be used in court proceedings. Penalties may be imposed upon spouses who obtain information in such a way. Similarly, it is forbidden to obtain documents which belong to the other spouse, have been locked away somewhere, are kept privately or, in the case of electronic documents, are on the spouse's computer or protected by passwords.

It is illegal to access other people's phones without consent. It is illegal to obtain an itemised bill for another person's phone. Secret phone bugging is illegal; so is computer hacking. These actions can land someone with criminal charges. Whenever I am told about such behaviour, I always advise the client not to do it - or, if it has been done, to stop it immediately. Nor is there any point in handing over the evidence to me - as I cannot look at it.

Human nature being what it is, they don't always stop. Somebody who is going through marital breakdown, who feels a need to know if their spouse is having an affair, often does not care about the possible consequences. Many of those in this situation do not realise that in the majority of circumstances, the law does not require people to go to such lengths – and indeed, forbids them from doing so.

In one case, Imerman v Tchenguiz & Others (2009), a wealthy businessman, who was estranged from his wife, sued his billionaire brothers-in-law. He claimed they had downloaded private information from a shared computer system without his authority, then misused that information by handing some of it to his wife and her lawyers. The information was deposited with the court after his wife began divorce proceedings.

The brothers contended their actions were taken *"in accordance with the administration of justice."* They argued that the businessman had no intention of making full and frank disclosure, that their sister was entitled to "equality of arms" and that her human rights required protection.

However there was no evidence that the husband had not intended to make full and frank disclosure. Furthermore, the brothers were not parties to the divorce. Predictably, their argument failed miserably in the High Court. The judge made the point that the brothers could not have legally obtained a court order for this information. He also reinforced the position that obtaining a search and seize order is only a remedy of last resort.

The following year the case came before the Court of Appeal, where judges ruled that the documents obtained in this way could not be used by the wife in her divorce case. They also declared there was no legal basis for the "Hildebrand Rules", which alarmed divorce lawyers up and down the country. Under the "Hildebrand Rules", clients were permitted to obtain copies of confidential information from a spouse, as long as force was not used. For example, there was nothing unlawful in copying a bank statement belonging to your spouse, if you found it lying in a drawer. It used to be understood that copies of documents "left lying around", could usually be produced without any legal problems. Since 2010, however, such activities have been forbidden. To date, the only exception to this rule appears to be if the spouse can argue that he or she has always had access to the documents in question.

One lawyer described the decision in the Imerman case as a "Cheat's Charter". And how many clients don't have any documents at all about their spouse? I would suggest very few if any. But because they are no longer supposed to have these documents, copy them, or discuss them with their own lawyers, even if they have been found or have simply left lying around in their home, they are supposed to replace them, and then conveniently forget about them and pretend they know nothing about them .

This decision, which from a practical perspective flies in the face of common sense, has significantly altered the balance of fairness between the spouses, and made life very tough indeed for clients who are married to duplicitous and secretive spouses.

If there is a genuine or urgent need to protect assets, documents or data, perfectly legal remedies are available. The costs you incur can be significant – but if your ex is playing dirty tricks, it is likely that he or she will end up having to pay them. The general rule is that there is no order for costs, but in a case such as this, that rule would probably not apply.

The court is always available to you, and legal remedies can include search and seize, ordering the protection or handover of documentation, or compelling a third party to give evidence. Sometimes, if the case requires it, a hearing may take place without the other side being aware of it. Judges are experienced lawyers and will want to ensure the stronger party doesn't pull a fast one. So don't despair. But before taking any steps you may later regret, get your own, fact-specific legal advice.

The Social Media Boom

Family lawyers are finding it difficult to ignore social media. Eight years ago, Friends Reunited was held responsible for the rising divorce rate as users contacted their former partners. More recently, Facebook and Twitter have been blamed. One 2011 survey of 5,000 divorce petitions claimed that a third of the behaviour petitions contained the word "Facebook". The most common reasons for citing Facebook related to the other party's behaviour with members of the opposite sex, but also parties using their public walls as divorce "weapons", post-separation. When Twitter appeared in petitions, it was for a similar reason: unpleasant comments about former partners.

Why are warring couples throwing caution to the wind and broadcasting their rage and revulsion towards one another online? Social networks can be addictive, particularly when fuelled by emotion or alcohol. They also tap into a common need that I often encounter with former partners, who feel compelled to keep contacting one another, even when they have nothing positive to say. Clients used to resort to text messages, which fulfilled the same need, but were at least private. Now it appears that Facebook and Twitter have taken over, with outcomes that are potentially more damaging.

It is true that in some divorce cases, Facebook and Twitter have their uses. For those in the public eye, Twitter can be viewed as a tool to "set the record straight".

However, small personal vindications can be far outweighed by the legal implications. What is said online can easily be stored, retrieved and presented in court at a later date. A courtroom may seem like a world away from a comfy armchair and an iPad, but it isn't. Not when the outcome could be an adverse decision in a child contact dispute, or an adverse settlement for divorce litigation misconduct. "Going public" in this way, and sending malicious communications around the world for everyone to see, could be counted as unreasonable behaviour for divorce and could result in various injunctions, child contact issues, financial awards and increased costs awards.

At its worst, a diatribe on Twitter or Facebook can cross the line into cyberbullying. In my experience as a family lawyer, online harassment in divorce cases is rarely reported on, but is becoming increasingly prevalent. Cyberbullying and harassment are criminal offences in England and Wales. However online abuse is often anonymous, and it can be difficult to ascertain the culprit's identity, even when the clues are all there, because websites are reluctant to provider users' details.

At the time of writing, there are plans for a Defamation Bill, which will reform libel laws and see a duty placed on internet service providers and websites to help identify those posting defamatory messages. This much-needed Bill, while not aimed squarely at divorce cases, nevertheless reflects how social media's role in divorce cases is set to become more prominent still. For this reason, we are currently advising all our clients to think long and hard before they press the "Post", "Tweet" or "Send" buttons.

Death

Every so often, something dreadfully unexpected happens in a divorce case: one of the parties dies. The chances of this are slim but when it happens, everything is thrown into turmoil. Unpleasant as it is, death is something you need to consider as the divorce process begins. You don't want to be left in serious legal and financial difficulties.

Firstly, you need to think about jointly-owned property when you are getting divorced. Most likely, you currently own it on the basis that one party automatically inherits in the event of the other's death. But when getting divorced you might want to change this, so that you leave it in your will to your nominated beneficiaries. This is called "severing joint tenancy". If you do decide to sever the joint tenancy, you must send a notice to your spouse indicating you have done this and you must register your notice at the Land Registry. Remember that severing the joint tenancy also means you won't automatically inherit your spouse's share of the property.

Secondly, you need to make a will. If you make a will before the decree absolute is granted, any bequest to your spouse will automatically fail afterwards, unless it is made in accordance with a court order. If you remarry, your entire will becomes void unless the will specifically states it is made in contemplation of remarriage. When you make your will, ensure you leave a sensible financial settlement to your spouse, to try and avoid arguments about your estate that could swallow much of it up in legal costs.

Thirdly, note that any claim by a deceased person dies with them. So if the case hasn't settled, the assets will stay as they were at the date of death.

Regardless of any will that has or hasn't been made, if there is a death the court may adjust the estate of the deceased between claimants such as a divorcing spouse, a previous spouse and children. Such a claim is subject to a time limit (six months from the grant of probate), so court proceedings must take place promptly. As previously mentioned, it makes sense to take advice about your will, the tax implications and life insurance. Life insurance can be written in trust and is therefore outside the estate for tax purposes, to help meet your various liabilities.

CASEBOOK

Mrs T was one half of a very grand couple. A vast estate was wholly owned by her in-laws' family trust, and "loaned" by the trustees to the relevant beneficiaries, who included Mrs T's husband. The couple enjoyed an enviable lifestyle during their marriage.

When they decided to divorce, Mr and Mrs T agreed how the assets would be split. However, the

---

husband died before the court had made an order that would have given Mrs T a "clean break" from him. Although they had come to a financial agreement, the couple had not yet received their decree absolute.

We were able to make a claim under the Inheritance Act. All the other beneficiaries under the trusts were amply provided for - and after a long negotiation, with the consent of all concerned, Mrs T obtained more than she had been about to receive in the divorce.

CASEBOOK

Mr O had children and had been married for a long time. He had fallen head-over-heels for another woman, and had left his wife. He felt guilty, but had made his choice. His financial settlement was generous: in return for no further maintenance liability to his wife, he paid over all his capital to her. This amounted to his interest in a modest house and some insurance policies which, in the event of his death, would provide for his family. He also agreed to pay generous maintenance to his children. He knew that he did not need to pay so much, but was committed to walking away from his marriage with the knowledge that his family was financially secure.

> *He bought a small house with his new partner. The purchase was funded by a capital payment from her, and a large mortgage with an insurance policy in place as security. Several years later he died in a road accident - and it emerged that Mr O had not made a will. The insurance policy paid off the mortgage in full. As he had owned the property with his new partner as 'beneficial joint tenants', his share of the house passed to her automatically. His former wife challenged this. She instructed solicitors to make a claim on behalf of the children.*
>
> *When we wrote back refuting the claim, however, she never issued proceedings. I suspect she was advised that she would fail. The court would have had a balancing exercise to make; given Mr O's new partner's contribution to the property, and to the mortgage and insurance policies, they would have likely made an order that allowed her to stay in her home. The former wife had already received a generous settlement that provided for her family.*

Incomplete paperwork

It may be tempting to bury your head in the sand, ignore the disputes over money and leave the whole process to the lawyers. But if you intend to remarry and you haven't been diligent with your paperwork, you may discover that being an ostrich has been a costly mistake. There is a nasty little technicality in the law, of which I suspect most people are totally unaware.

The often long and drawn-out process of receiving a financial settlement begins with a simple, procedural matter. This happens in some cases but not all. You complete a financial application and lodge it immediately with the court with an associated fee. If you fail to do this before you remarry, you may not be able to make a financial claim against your former spouse - ever.

At Stowe Family Law we have a clause in our retainer letter, stating that if a client intends to remarry they must tell us beforehand, because it can affect the client's entitlement to a settlement.

Similarly, some couples never bother to obtain an order resolving their finances. They think a divorce is all they need. But consider this. Some years later, one of the former partners wins the Lottery or sells a business. Because those respective claims are still open and haven't been closed off, either party may still claim against the other. The court will consider that couple's finances at the date of the hearing, not the date of their separation or divorce. You have been warned!

CASEBOOK

One of my solicitors rushed into the office in a panic to tell me that one of our clients, Mrs N, was getting remarried the following week. She had been divorced by her first husband, but as yet there was no financial settlement between them. He was very wealthy and was making no claim against her. All the assets were up for discussion between the par-

ties and there was going to be a big payout to her by the husband.

Mrs N, not wishing to be seen as a gold digger - particularly as she'd had an affair with another man - had expressly refused us permission to issue a financial application. She had instructed us that every attempt should be made to resolve matters amicably. Negotiations were still ongoing between the couple. Because she was the respondent, all she had to do to obtain a divorce was to complete an "Acknowledgement of Service", confirming receipt of the petition and various other matters.

As it turned out, the husband had guessed that the wife was intending to remarry. Knowing this, and having been advised he had not issued a financial application himself, he hoped she would fall into the waiting trap and find herself unable to make a claim against him. His plan failed. Our client retainer specifically refers to remarriage and asks clients to notify us if they intend to remarry.

We rallied into action and quickly issued her Form A, seeking a lump sum order against her former husband. My client remarried as planned the following week and eventually her case settled. She was still able to go to court after the remarriage and seek her settlement. Had she not informed us of her forthcoming wedding, she may not have been so lucky. The financial contribution she made to her

20-year marriage could have gone unrecognised.

In another case, not one of ours, the court "saved" a husband from the remarriage trap. It was decided that because the wife had made a financial claim within the divorce petition, this gave the court jurisdiction to make an award on the husband's behalf. In our case, there was no such application. It is far better to be safe than sorry.

I always advise anyone intending to remarry to tell their solicitor in good time. That way, they can be fully advised about the consequences and the necessary processes can be implemented.

Agreement falls apart at the 11th hour

You may reach an agreement, only to change your mind. What happens next?

If you wish to pull out of an agreement before there is formal documentation of any kind, you can do so. At this stage you are negotiating your settlement. The courts encourage "without prejudice" negotiations, meaning that you can make your offers and counter-offers without being bound to them.

If there is formal written evidence of your concluded agreement, you may be held to it. Never allow anything to be put formally in writing until you are 100 per cent sure about your decision and it has been thoroughly discussed with and checked by your lawyers. You do not want to find yourself held to an unwanted agreement, signed under pressure from your spouse. Don't let yourself be talked or rushed into anything.

Your circumstances change after a settlement has been finalised.

If you have settled against legal advice, then there is probably nothing you can do about it later. So if your lawyer is urging you not to settle, and you do and then decide later on you wish you had taken that advice it will be very difficult to do anything about it.

Let's take one high-profile case as an example. A 2009 headline in The Daily Mail read: *"Husband who became millionaire AFTER divorce not obliged to give ex wife more money, judges rule"*. This was the case of Walkden v Walkden, heard in the Court of Appeal.

The judgment had important implications for all parties and their lawyers, because it all but removed the safety net to set aside court orders. Although it is not my practice to comment publicly on named clients' cases, here is an exception, and I will refer only to facts that are already in the public domain. I would stress that the advice and client examples I give thereafter are not connected with the Walkden case.

One of our solicitors at Stowe Family Law represented Mrs Walkden and, I am pleased to say, assisted her to reach the financial compromise in advance of the Court of Appeal's ruling. The details of the case are as follows:

- **Mr and Mrs Walkden divorced in 2006.** The husband's timber company was valued, and split 58:42 in his favour. Mrs Walkden received a fixed settlement of around £482,000 and ongoing maintenance of £1,100 a month. Case closed? Not quite.
- **Less than three months after the divorce settle-**

ment was finalised, the husband's company was sold for more than £3,700,000 – an amount that far exceeded the original valuation. In effect, that 58:42 split became 82:18.

- **The county court gave Mrs Walkden permission to return to court** to seek an increased settlement, on the basis that a "new event" had occurred.
- **In the judgment handed down,** the court set out the law in great detail, leaving no-one in any doubt about their views. The court found that Mr Walkden was not obliged to make additional provision for his former wife

In any such case, the first question to be asked is whether an agreement has been rendered invalid by misrepresentation, mistake, breach of duty of full frank and clear disclosure, fraud or undue influence. In this case, the court found the agreement had not been rendered invalid. The court also found that if clear legal advice is given and the client chooses to ignore it, then she cannot complain afterwards.

The judge said that while he did not wish parties to be deterred from entering into an agreement, any such settlement *"if properly arrived at is likely to be binding and the opportunities to unravel it will be limited in the extreme."*

There we have it, loud and clear, from the Court of Appeal. You cannot return to court easily or at all. You certainly can't complain if assets turn out to be worth far more or far less than you think. At the time of writing it is almost impossible to set aside a court order. Fraud could provide grounds, but is very, very hard to prove. I have done it in the past, when a husband told his wife that an asset was worthless, when in fact it was worth £1.5 million at the time he made the statement. The fraud was difficult to prove and very expensive. In the end we got there, but by the skin of our teeth!

You ignore advice

You may be "king of the castle" elsewhere, but this does not - repeat not - make you a clued-up divorce lawyer, forensic accountant or commercial valuer. So please don't close your mind to sound advice in order to do the deal "your way". You may regret it. Countless times new clients have said to me, having had time to reflect on their actions, *"I wish I had seen you first."* Or, when there is nothing more to be done: "I wish I had listened!" Remember: you get one chance only. Your decision will affect you for the rest of your life. Please don't blow it.

In a similar vein, don't be ridiculously generous! Sometimes a husband or wife feels guilty about events during the marriage and, as a result, is prepared to over-compensate or accept an unnecessarily modest settlement. Once the divorce has been concluded and emotions are no longer running high, such decisions can be regretted for years afterwards. Sadly, it is too late by then and nothing can be done about it.

If you are paying for advice, take it. If your advisers recommend a professional valuation from qualified valuers, they are doing so in your interests. Obtain one.

Let's say your spouse gives you a valuation of their company, prepared by accountants. It looks ok to you. Your spouse offers you half this figure. You accept and breathe a sigh of relief that everything is agreed so easily. However, did you know there are several different ways of valuing a business?

Has the correct method been adopted here? Did you know that properties may be included at values that are years out of date? Did you know that sometimes, business interests are discounted by a significant percentage, when a discount may not be applied by the court at all?

You didn't know? Exactly!

If you still refuse to agree to a valuation, and your advisers produce letters for you to sign, indemnifying and absolving them from any liability in the event that things go pear-shaped for you, you should start to worry. Clearly, your advisers are so concerned about your steadfast decisions, they naturally want to protect themselves in case you decide to sue them in the future.

Financial Dispute Resolution: when your spouse twists the thumbscrews

In _chapter 17_ I described the Financial Dispute Resolution (FDR) hearing, in which the parties are provided the opportunity to settle their case on a "Without Prejudice" basis, similar to mediation. I usually welcome these hearings. However I have noticed a disturbing trend, to which I referred in chapter 17 and which I would like to explore in greater detail here.

The pressure to achieve a successful outcome, together with new rules that require parties to pay their own costs, have become useful weapons in the unscrupulous spouse's armoury.

It is worth bearing in mind that because judges are accustomed to an adversarial system, they don't always approach FDRs as mediators. Many judges are excellent; however, if a judge does not use his or her skills to persuade the parties to negotiate, or to issue wake-up calls when necessary, an FDR can be a fruitless and expensive waste of time.

I also think that in some cases, judges can be a little naïve when spouses decide to play a dirtier game. This can happen when a wealthier spouse – and let's say it is the husband – makes his wife a deliberately low offer. For example, he may try to obtain a clean break rather than an agreement to pay maintenance, even when a clean break would be a highly unlikely outcome in court.

He knows his offer is too low, but he believes that he has little to lose. He can either force his wife into accepting the offer, because she is terrified about her mounting legal costs and the length of time it will take for the court hearing to take place, or he can force her to litigate and realise all those fears. If she litigates and he is ordered to pay her a greater sum, the only downside is his increased costs – and let's remember, the wife still has her own bill to pay. For her, it can be a crushing defeat or a pyrrhic victory; for him, it can be a gamble he is prepared to take.

As the economy has worsened, I have observed an increased number of such "gambles". These can pose problems for judges. After all, faced with a commercially-minded, hard-headed litigant who is determined to push the other party into a corner, what can the court do? Very little, it seems. The court can merely conclude the FDR and make orders for the case to head for a final hearing.

In one case that I observed recently, the husband pulled this trick and the judge responded with a fruitless attempt to find some middle ground. But this middle ground suited no-one: the husband wouldn't countenance it, and it came nowhere near what the wife was seeking. The judge did not give the husband the "hard word" to encourage him to move towards a financial settlement. So the husband left the court as he entered it: intending to take the case to a final hearing if necessary, but convinced that his wife will settle with him beforehand.

There are those who would argue that costs consequences may still arise if there is a failure to make sensible open proposals. However, judges are more likely to regard this as an exceptional course of action rather than the norm.

If you are heading for a FDR I wish you well, but please be aware of these potential pitfalls. When these hearings work, they work extremely well. However, it does concern me when spouses attempt to "game" them in the way that I have outlined above. In my opinion it is a failing of the system that needs to be remedied.

Part VIII: How to Move On

30: So I'm Divorced. Now What?

You're all done? Congratulations! You have freedom and choices. You cannot know if the path ahead will be smooth, but at least you are moving in a forward direction.

Your decree absolute will land on your doormat, sent by your solicitor. It is a low-key end to an emotionally turbulent time in your life. Keep the decree absolute in a safe place, because if you remarry, you will need to produce the original copy.

For now, there remain a number of practical and emotional matters for you to consider. This section of the book will help you to do that.

Checklist: Practical Matters

1. **Are you changing your surname?** Sometimes wives wish to do so, and it's an easy process. All you need to do is complete a statutory declaration or deed poll. A solicitor can help you, or your local Citizens Advice Bureau can advise further. As previously noted, if you wish to change your children's surnames you will need permission of the children's father or an order of the court, which is rarely granted.

2. **Have you informed your children's schools that the divorce has been finalised?** Schools should be kept up-to-date so that they can monitor your children and give them extra care and support, if necessary.

3. **Have you changed your will?** I have mentioned this earlier, but I don't think I can remind you about it enough!

4. **Your old will should be changed if it makes reference to a former spouse,** although any bequest to a former spouse would automatically fail unless the will made it clear the provision was to last following the decree absolute. Please also remember that if you re-marry, any will made before remarriage will be invalid.

5. **Have you applied for a new passport, bearing your new details?** Visit www.ips.gov.uk for further information.

6. **Have you informed your mortgage lender of any changed details or relevant developments?**

7. **Have you closed any joint bank accounts, as per the court order?**

8. **Have you changed the personal contact details on any remaining bank accounts and credit cards?** Some banks will allow you to do this over the telephone; others will insist on a face-to-face meeting and supporting documentation such as your decree absolute and utilities bills.

9. **Have you applied for a new driver's licence, bearing your new details?** Visit www.dvla.gov.uk for further information. Failure to do this could result in a fine.

10. **Have you updated the details on any relevant insurance policies?**

11. **Have you notified Her Majesty's Revenue & Customs of your new situation and contact de-**

tails? Visit www.hmrc.gov.uk for further information.

12. **Have you updated the relevant details on telephone and utilities bills?** These could range from changed correspondence details to new friends and family numbers.

13. **Where applicable: have you visited your local benefits office, to discover what you may now be entitled to claim?** Visit www.dwp.gov.uk/contactus for further information.

14. **Have you signed the necessary forms** to resign from any business assets in which you previously had an interest?

Your top nine challenges

Dear Marilyn

Being on my own like this makes me feel strange. I broke up with my husband six months ago and so technically, I've been on my own for a while now. But it is only since the divorce came through that it has really hit home! I am sure I used to get many more social invitations when I was one half of a couple. When the kids see their dad I'm left alone in the house, and even the peace and quiet make me feel uncomfortable. I don't feel like myself anymore. Is this normal?

Bella

Dear Bella,

The stress of a divorce cannot be underestimated. When the case is over, it can be like the lid coming off the top of a pressure cooker. In my experience, people are particularly vulnerable at this time. They can feel lonely and sad. Mood swings, panic attacks and depression are all normal.

Now it is time for you to rebuild your life. Take things day by day, step by step. Above all, don't keep glancing towards the past and wondering, "what if?" You have already hit the bottom: now the only way is up.

Marilyn

There are challenges that you are likely to encounter over the course of the coming year. There are no right or wrong answers, but you can try to ensure a smoother journey. I asked Julie Levine, counsellor at the Oakdale Centre in Harrogate (contact details at the back of this book) to assist me with insights and advice for the following situations:

1. **Filling out forms.** This sounds like a minor issue, but it is one that many of my newly separated and divorced clients find unexpectedly difficult. From now on, whenever a form asks for your marital status you will tick the "Divorced" box or the "Separated" box. You don't go back to ticking the "Single" box. You may see this as an admission of failure, or it may raise the question, *"who*

am I?" Perhaps you are happy to think of yourself as divorced or separated; if you are not, remember that you have embarked on a new journey and take things as they come.

2. **Valentine's Day.** If you find yourself on your own on Valentine's Day, you may be depressed if you are used to a romantic evening or away break at that time of year. There is no quick fix, but please understand that by the same time next year, you will have made progress towards becoming whole again.

3. **Christmas.** In *chapter 25* I suggested some pointers to make Christmas enjoyable for your children. But what about you? What if you spend Christmas away from your children? Many families alternate Christmases between parents. If you still have an amicable relationship with your former spouse or you are both sufficiently mature to put the children's needs first, you may still be able to enjoy Christmases together.

4. **Your wedding anniversary.** Some couples don't stand on ceremony on this date, but if you are used to being fussed over on your "special day" – or even if you see it as the date when your life took a wrong turn - you must now be prepared to let it blend back into the other anonymous days of the year. For some people, anniversaries will remind them that what they had is gone. Some people will be relieved. How others feel will depend on how well they are coming to terms with what has happened. The first year is always horrible, the second year is less painful and the third and fourth years are less painful still. Give it time.

5. **Emergency childcare.** If an emergency arises at home and you have to leave the house suddenly, or if a situation develops at work and you are late getting away, what do you do about the children? This may not have been a problem when there were two adults living at home, but now you must look further afield. If none of your children's grandparents, aunts and uncles live nearby, upon whom can you call? Keep a list of numbers at home and at work; if you want to avoid impossible situations, it is best to be prepared. Stay on good terms with your neighbours – you may need their help in a pinch.

6. **Shared friends.** When you were a couple, you probably moved in similar social circles and shared a number of friends. Now those friends may have to choose – or feel they have to choose – between you and your former partner. When some of them align themselves with your former partner, you may feel hurt and rejected. One tragedy of divorce is that you find out who your friends are and aren't. It can be excruciating, but you will soon learn who you can trust. Accept that other friends have stuck by you, and value those friendships.

7. **Dinner parties.** From now on you may experience "Bridget Jones Syndrome" at dinner parties and other social events: becoming an object of pity and curiosity, in a room packed with "smug marrieds". People may try to set you up, which can be uncomfortable. What you do is down to you. Can you handle such a situation? How emotionally competent are you feeling? If you do not feel ready, don't go.

8. **Introducing a new partner to friends and family members.** This situation must be negotiated with care. Julie recommends that new partners are first introduced to your children, when the time is appropriate. This is because your children are on your "frontline". If they are accepting of your new partner, your parents may be too. After all, everyone wants the children to be happy! Introductions to friends should be more straightforward, especially if your friends have been playing matchmakers.

9. **Internet dating.** Many people find partners online. If you try internet dating, make sure you are emotionally ready for it. It is likely you will dating, make sure that you are emotionally ready for it. d who introduced.

Dear Marilyn

I am 30 and I don't know if I can ever fall in love again. My last relationship ended disastrously, and I found it difficult to cope. I am determined that what happened will never be repeated. If I am going to be alone for the rest of my life, so be it. There's nothing wrong with that, is there?

Jenny

Dear Jenny,

You are so young! You are bound to feel down. I think it is wrong to concentrate on whether you will or won't have a relationship. Relax! There's so much going on in the world. Look for other things in life and forget about a new relationship until you are ready. Although you think right now it won't, experience suggests otherwise. Many of my clients bump into me years later, and tell me how they doubted the same advice I gave to them, but realised I was right after all! In the meantime, exercise. Think about improving your mind and body. Stretch yourself in areas that are new and exciting.

Finally, a thought. What have you taken away from your last relationship? Why didn't it work? If you know the answers, you can move forward with confidence.

Marilyn

31: Setting Yourself Goals for the Future

Put your past behind you, and you can move on with your life. By the time you read this, your spouse or partner will no longer be around, and the papers will have been signed, sealed and delivered. It's a perfect time to begin moving forward!

The previous chapter covered the niggles and challenges that are all part and parcel of beginning a fresh page in your life. Think of this chapter as my suggestions to inject a breeze of fresh air. Take a notebook and fill out the answers to this simple worksheet, to help you consider your future and make your days as rewarding and enjoyable as possible. Take your time - but it would be great if you could set some goals, wouldn't it?

Worksheet: Make the most of your free time

- **Which places have you always wanted to visit?** Perhaps you did not have time before, or perhaps your former partner displayed little enthusiasm for such trips. These places could be far-flung destinations; they could be small attractions or landmarks close to home. List three of them. You could go with a companion, or your children; or you may choose to travel alone. As you visit each place in turn, mark it off with the date(s) of your trip.

- **Have you lost touch, or almost lost touch, with any of your close friends or former colleagues?** Now is the time to rekindle these relationships. List three of them, get in touch for a chat and mark the dates.

- **List your three favourite, long lost foods.** These

could be ingredients, products or dishes. What they must all have in common is (a) you adore them, and (b) you haven't cooked or eaten them for a long time. Perhaps your former partner didn't like them, or perhaps you were simply caught up elsewhere. Alternatively, list foods that you have always wanted to try, and never have. The most exquisite cake in the baker's window, perhaps, or a dish that did not suit your former partner's dietary regime. As you polish off each one, mark the date.

- **Are there any activities that you have always wanted to try or take up, but never have?** Now's the time. What's more, new experiences can often lead to new friends. Perhaps you have always wanted to volunteer, or join a particular community group. Or perhaps you have always wanted to take up a sport such as golf, or snowboarding. List three of these activities. As you try each one for the first time, mark the date.
- **What books have you always wanted to read?** List three of them, and mark them off as you read them.
- **At this stage in your life, how would you like to improve yourself?** Your ideas for self-improvement could range from a brave new haircut to a personal development course. List three of your ideas, and mark them off as you do them.
- **When you have filled out all of these lists, look back at them.** What a lot of accomplishments and achievements are here! Every one of them represents another step on the path to the person that you will become, rather than the person you were. Isn't the future looking better already?

Closing Remarks

Sometimes I am asked if I like being a family lawyer. It is an easy question to answer. I like people, I very much like helping people and I'm a keen observer of human nature. I think it helps me in my own efforts to improve myself as a person.

I encounter situations that arise out of human fallibility, and I try hard to prevent others from going down the same tough roads.

People may look different from one another, and speak different languages, but in my experience we are created to think and feel along the same lines.

Within their individual boundaries, people share an understanding and appreciation of good and bad, moral and immoral. With our thoughts, desires and actions, none of us can claim to be anything other than fallible - even though we may sometimes think we know all the arguments and the answers.

It is this same fallibility, and the realisation that dawns when people don't have answers to questions they don't understand, which gives rise to the problems presented to me. The causes of the problems are often the same, brought about as they are by failed relationships. The client, unable to control emotions and perceived needs, becomes lost in a terrifying, chaotic situation.

Emotions are so difficult to control. For someone stuck in the sameness of an everyday routine, a sudden encounter with the strongest of emotions can result in a decision to throw caution to the winds. The power of that emotion can knock a person off-balance forever.

I have witnessed, and come to respect, the raw power of emotion on both sides of a divorce. Often things are said that are not meant, or things remain unsaid. When this happens, the situation can worsen. Sometimes, when clients crave for more in their lives, I advise them to be grateful for the sameness of an everyday routine.

Over the years I have witnessed and, I hope, helped more than ten thousand people to cope with the trauma of family breakdown. I encourage my clients to concentrate on the positive, rather than the negative. Even when events and emotions are difficult to face, the best remedy is always to concentrate on forgetting the past, however difficult that may be.

It is my hope that Divorce & Splitting Up has proved to be a valuable resource during this testing period of your life. Support is always available to you; you just have to know where to look for it.

The Useful Resources section that follows lists a host of organisations, groups and services that can help you, if you are inclined to call upon them. The Stowe Family Law offices can be reached on +44 (0)1423 532600. My blog, www.marilyn-stowe.co.uk, is updated every day and features case studies, how-to guides and all the latest developments in family law. Please draw upon it because it will help you get the most out of this book.

Divorce is a contentious subject: its nature and procedures arouse passions in people and it is extremely difficult to find a consensus. I do not believe that divorce should be made more "difficult" and, contrary to some, I do not believe that there is much wrong with the way in which assets are divided under English law. At present our judges are permitted to use a certain amount of "judicial discretion" but, in years to come, family law may be made more "rigid", to bring it more into line with family law elsewhere in Europe. I fear that such rigidity would introduce unfairness and uncertainty. At the time of writing government cuts are about to smash the legal aid budget into smithereens.

It will be a great pity if such measures are introduced because, in my opinion, we currently enjoy the finest legal system in the world. It isn't perfect, but it does cater for the underdog. If such a system is distorted out of all recognition, it will be a sad day.

I am not going to wish you luck for the future - because I don't think that you are going to need it – but I do wish you all the best.

After all, this is the point at which the rest of your life begins.

Useful Resources

SERVICES AND HELPLINES

London
Stowe Family Law LLP, 8 Fulwood Place,
Gray's Inn, London WC1V 6HG
T: 020 7421 3300

Harrogate
Stowe Family Law LLP, Old Court House, Raglan Street,
Harrogate, North Yorkshire HG1 1LT
01423 532600

Cheshire
Stowe Family Law LLP, The Camellia Building, 38 Oxford
Road, Hale, Altrincham WA14 2EB
0161 926 1410

Wilmslow
92 Water Lane, Wilmslow, Cheshire SK9 5BB
01625 544900

Leeds
Stowe Family Law LLP, Portland House,
5 Portland Street, Leeds LS1 3DR
0113 224 0580

W: www.stowefamilylaw.co.uk
E: chiefexecutive@stowefamilylaw.co.uk

*Our firm is the largest specialist family law firm in the
country. If you are considering divorce or separation,
please don't hesitate to give us a call.*

Stowe Family Law Settlements

0844 854 5421

info@sflsettlements.co.uk

Stowe Family Law's partner firm, combining mediation with family law expertise. If your case is suitable for family mediation, Stowe Family Law Settlements' lawyer mediators will meet with you and your former partner at one of our offices. They will discuss the likely outcome of your case if it went to court, help both of you to decide upon the best possible solution and draw up a formal agreement.

Association for Shared Parenting

01789 751157

www.sharedparenting.org.uk

Charity that gives support and advice to fathers and mothers who are worried about the welfare of their children after a separation or divorce .It can also advise on some legal issues.

Child Maintenance Options

0800 988 0988

www.cmoptions.org

Service provided by the Child Maintenance Group, which is part of the Department for Work and Pensions. Child Maintenance Options provides impartial support to help both parents make informed choices about child maintenance. It also offers practical information in areas linked to child maintenance, such as housing, employment and money.

Citizens Advice

England: 08444 111 444

Wales: 08444 77 20 20

www.citizensadvice.org.uk

Free, confidential advice service which helps people with legal and financial problems.

Community Legal Advice
0845 345 4345
www.gov.uk
Assess your eligibility for legal aid.

DirectGov
www.direct.gov.uk
The government's information website is the first port of call for anybody who wants a "Do It Yourself" divorce. It provides sound, basic information.

Disabled Parents Network
0300 3300 639
www.disabledparentsnetwork.org.uk
Support, information and advice for disabled parents and their families.

Family Mediation Helpline
0845 602 6627
www.familymediationhelpline.co.uk
Provides general information and details of mediation services in your area

Families Need Fathers
0870 7607 496 (helpline)
www.fnf.org.uk
Campaigning organisation, which supports parents who are worried about not seeing their children. Its services are also available to extended family members.

Gingerbread
020 7403 9500 (enquiries)
0800 018 4318 (single parent helpline)
www.gingerbread.org.uk
Charity supporting lone parents and their children.

Jewish Marriage Council
020 8203 6311 (enquiries and counselling)
www.jmc-uk.org
Offers relationship counselling to Jewish couples and families.

Law Society Family Law Panel
www.accreditation.sra.org.uk
Accredited solicitors have had their knowledge and experience in family law assessed.

Legal Ombudsman for England and Wales
0300 555 0333
www.legalombudsman.org.uk
Service set up by Parliament, with formal powers to investigate and resolve complaints about lawyers.

Men's Advice Line
0808 801 0327
www.mensadviceline.org.uk
Confidential helpline, providing support and practical advice for men who have experienced or who are experiencing domestic abuse.

NACSA
01384 572525
www.nacsa.co.uk
Campaigning organisation, which provides support to parents who are struggling with the CSA.

National Debtline
0800 138 5445
Free, confidential debt advice.

National Domestic Violence Helpline
0808 2000 247
www.womensaid.org.uk
This free, confidential helpline is run by Women's Aid, the

key national charity working to end domestic violence against women and children in the UK.

National Family Mediation
01392 271 610
www.nfm.orf.uk
A network of not-for-profit Family Mediation Services.

Oakdale Centre Counselling
01423 503080
www.theoakdalecentre.co.uk
Harrogate-based service that can help with relationship counselling, personal counselling and working with families on child contact arrangements.

Parentline Plus
0808 800 2222
www.parentlineplus.org.uk
Free parenting advice and support, 24/7.

Pink Therapy
020 7434 0367
www.pinktherapy.com
The UK's largest independent therapy organisation working with gender and sexual minority clients. London-based.

Relate
0300 100 1234 (appointments booking line)
www.relate.org.uk
Relate offers relationship counselling, sex therapy, workshops, mediation and support. At the time of writing, a 60 minute telephone counselling session costs £45.

Resolution
01689 820272
www.resolution.org.uk
Organisation of 5,000 lawyers, who advocate mediation and collaborative divorce.

Respect
0845 122 8609 (information and advice for people who are
abusive towards their partners)
0808 801 0327 (confidential advice line for men experiencing domestic abuse)
www.respect.uk.net
www.mensadviceline.org.uk
*Membership association, which supports abusive men and
women who wish to change their behaviour. It also manag-
es a confidential advice line for abused men.*

Websites and Blogs

Marilyn Stowe's blog: www.marilynstowe.co.uk
*My blog, which is regularly updated, features case studies,
how-to guides and all the latest developments in family law.*

Couples in Europe: www.coupleseurope.eu
*This useful website sets out the law for couples in all 27 EU
countries.*

Family Lore: www.familylore.co.uk
A blog by English family lawyer John Bolch.

First Wives' World: www.firstwivesworld.com
*A women's social network, which also provides divorce-re-
lated news and advice.*

Getting Your Get: www.gettingyourget.co.uk
A free guide to Jewish divorce.

The Ministry of Justice: www.justice.gov.uk
Download court forms from the link at this site.

Wikivorce: www.wikivorce.com
A bustling and informative divorce support community.

Acknowledgements

If I listed all of those who have given so generously of their love, help and support, this book would have an extra chapter.

However I would like to thank my dedicated colleagues and friends at Stowe Family Law, for all they have done and continue to do, particularly all those who have contributed to this book. I would like to thank all those who were also members of our firm when it was still part of Grahame Stowe Bateson. It was 30 years ago when Stowe Family Law began life in a converted cobblers' shop in Halton, Leeds. We have come a long way together.

I am humbled by the faith and support of my clients, who have put their faith and trust in me and to whom I remain eternally grateful. I extend my most sincere thanks to them all.

Karyn Fleeting, I am very grateful for all your hard work. This book would not have been possible in its highly professional form without you.

Julie Lavine: thank you for your wise words and contribution.

My parents, sister and brother deserve special thanks for their heartfelt support at different times, always showing their love, throughout the years. Mum and Dad, where would I have been without you? I wouldn't have been a lawyer, that's for sure!

Last but by no means least, from the bottom of my heart I would like to thank the two marvellous men who make my life complete: my "senior partner", who continues to put up with my ways (I am certain that his complaints are in jest!) and our darling Ben, who continues to give overriding purpose to our lives and whose talents and achievements, we are certain, will far surpass our own.

To you all, this book is dedicated with all my love.

Index

Affair   19, 20-21, 23-27

Arbitration   75-77

Bankruptcy   218

CAFCASS   231-232

Child Maintenance Options
      240-241

Child support   238-252

Children
      99-101, 142-148, 221-269

Children Act 1989   225-226

Christmas   24-36

Civil partnerships
      55, 127-129

Clean break   182-192

Cohabiting couples
      60, 114-126

Collaborative divorce   69-70

Conflicting out   93-95

Contact order
      226-227, 275-277

Costs   214-220

Counselling   46, 105-106

Court hearing
      174-176, 286-287

CSA   241-248, 250-252

Death   293-296

Deed of separation   49

Divorce
      16-17, 52-59, 130-131

Divorce loan   218-219

DIY divorce   10, 68-69

Domestic violence   38-42

Domicile   139

Duxbury Tables   160-161

Emotions   102

Enforcement order 258-259

Fathers' rights   253-260

"Faux Friends"   110-113

Financial Dispute
Resolution 171-174, 303-305

Financial settlement
      67, 177-178

First appointment
      86-91, 169-171

Forensic accountant
      205-207

Fraud   210-213

Form E   92, 178-179

"Forum shopping"   64

Gow v Grant   124-126

Grandparents' rights
270-280

Hague Convention on Child
Abduction   143-145, 146

Hidden assets   202-213

Hildebrand Rules   289-290

House   161-165

Imerman v Tchenguiz
& Others   289-290

International divorce
132-148

Legal aid   8

Lone parents   235-236

Maintenance
159-161, 180-182

"Man-o-Pause"   30

"Mareva" injunction   140

Marriage mantras   36

Matrimonial Causes
Act 1973, Section 25   151

Mediation   70-73

Mesher order   217-218

MIAM   73

Money   62-63, 149-192

Non-molestation order   41

Occupation order   41

Parental responsibility
224-225

Payne v Payne   145-148

Pension planning   165-168

Prenuptial
agreement   11, 64, 193-201

Prohibited steps order   227

Radmacher v Granatino
11, 193

Relationship rescue   29

Remarriage   297-299

Residence order   226

Sears Tooth agreement
219-220

Separation   48-50

Shared parenting   148

Shared residence order   228

Solicitors   67, 77-86, 96-98

Snooping   19, 288-291

Social media   291-293

Specific issue order   227

Surnames   237, 306

Walkden v Walkden
300-301

White v White   64